The Psychic Way

Fine-tuning Your Intuition

The Psychic Way

Fine-tuning Your Intuition

Barbara Ford-Hammond

Winchester, UK
Washington, USA

First published by Sixth Books, 2011
Sixth Books is an imprint of John Hunt Publishing Ltd., Laurel House, Station Approach,
Alresford, Hants, SO24 9JH, UK
office1@o-books.net
www.o-books.com

For distributor details and how to order please visit the 'Ordering' section on our website.

Text copyright: Barbara Ford-Hammond 2010

ISBN: 978 1 84694 721 6

A CIP catalogue record for this book is available from the British Library.

Design: Stuart Davies

Printed in the UK by CPI Antony Rowe
Printed in the USA by Offset Paperback Mfrs, Inc

We operate a distinctive and ethical publishing philosophy in all
areas of our business, from our global network of authors to
production and worldwide distribution.

CONTENTS

For You

Foreword

When I first told Barbara about my irrational fear of walking over high bridges, she said she could cure me of that phobia, easy peasy. Yeah, right, I thought, but having just read her latest book The Psychic Way, I believe her!

In my opinion, Barbara Ford Hammond is the real thing. A natural healer, psychic and friend to all who cross her path, and she encourages and teaches us to be the same, while remaining completely down to earth.

The Psychic Way is educational and inspirational. It helps us to go deep within ourselves searching for that special magic Barb knows is there. There is so much in this book, for everyone, and if you are reading this now you have obviously been guided to the Psychic Way because there is something in it for you.

For me, there is so much - I especially enjoyed Chapter 8: Spirit Guides and Angels, and Chapter 9: The Clairs. I believe I must be clairsentient.

I enjoy the way Barb writes – no frills, like when she describes a Native American Indian watching you 'scratch your bum'. What a visual! I laughed out loud!

This is a book to keep close, on your bedside table, on your desk, someplace it is easy to reach because you will want to constantly refer to it – as I have been doing.

My irrational fear of heights remains so I shall be calling Barbara soon to make an appointment. I wonder what I shall learn about myself ?

Meanwhile, I'll try some meditation, as in Chapter 18.

Bruna Zanelli – Journalist and author.

Introductory Musings

It's all make believe, isn't it?
Marilyn Monroe

Living the psychic way means different things to different people as I have discovered each time I've mentioned the title of this book. For me, it is a way of life: trusting intuition, being in the flow and trying to be helpful to others. It isn't always easy but when you 'get it' it is blissful.

Working as a hypnotist, muse and intuit tends to instigate interesting reactions when I first meet people. Occasionally, I am offered a wry smile; sometimes they back away making the sign of the cross, but mostly I get questioned for more information. However, when I started my hypnotherapy practice, my esoteric inclinations were not out in the open but they refused to remain hidden and niggled and poked until I acknowledged their presence, let them out to play and began to live the psychic way.

While this was happening many of my clients noticed that after their sessions they became more intuitive and psychic, which led me to create my Beyond Bliss workshops and retreats as a fun way to 'try out' and develop various skills. The contents of these classes range from seeing auras to dowsing, looking into your future to hypnotism and with so much in-between there is something for everyone.

The Psychic Way – Fine-tuning Your Intuition is based on Beyond Bliss and shows how, by practicing hypnotic meditation combined with a mix of techniques, you can develop your inner skills and improve your well-being. The book does not deliver a one size fits all approach but more a toolbox to dip into while discovering your fortes.

I believe that we all have natural but often hidden or ignored abilities and talents that are tucked away in our psyches. A lot of the time these skills are usually out of sight as many people have decided that our sixth sense and innate gifts should be ignored. Personally, I have my magical life and scientific interests sitting together very nicely with absolute respect for each other, clash-free and with many crossovers.

Through the years in my practice many people would see me when they had decided that 'enough was enough' with whatever issue or difficulty they were facing. At the moment they made contact with me they were making a choice to change their future. Eventually, after it dawned on me that we really do create our own successes, I became very excited and a little nervous. I mused that if we have the power and ability to create all that we see from inside our heads; why is it so hard to imagine that we can harness that power in ourselves? It is then one further little step that puts us in tune with everyone else. With your awareness switched on, by acknowledging and developing your psychic powers and intuition, you can create the life you truly desire.

You are responsible for what goes on in your mind. Only you. Others might try to influence you but unless drugs or brain-washing are involved you have the ultimate control of you. When you accept full awareness of yourself and the power within your own mind, practically anything is achievable. The only limitations are those imposed by you.

Many of my clients have had their 'Eureka!' moments of exactly what to do next in their lives while they were in hypnosis with direct access to their creative selves. This showed me that the quickest and easiest way to discover your innate skills is to use hypnotic techniques as a precursor to enhancing your intuitive abilities. This enables your mind to operate clearly without interference from your doubting thoughts or your inner chatterbox.

In this book you will learn how to use hypnotic meditation on yourself and others. You will be able to pop into and out of a trance whenever you like.

You will understand the inner workings of the mind.

You will be able to trust your intuition in all situations.

Think for a moment about the following:

When the phone rings do you ever sense who is calling?

Do people, sometimes strangers, automatically share personal knowledge with you?

Have you ever thought of someone you hadn't seen in ages only for them to call or email?

Are you a natural healer?

Can you sense if someone is ill?

Have you had premonitions that prove to be correct?

Do you see shadows or sense movement just out of sight at the corner of your eyes?

Do you have déjà vu moments?

Do animals like you?

If you said yes to some of these examples, you are probably already aware of your skills. This though is just the tip of the iceberg, as you will discover with the growth of your expertise.

We are all intuitive beings but some tend to shy away from anything not deemed 'normal' for fear of being labeled a new-age fluff ball or a purple character. I can assure you that I've been there. Entrepreneurs have a strong self-belief and are able to harness their inner power and focus their mind on the goal even if deals don't look particularly good at the outset. This is referred to as going with their gut or having a 'knack'. I believe we all have that knack; it just needs locating and freeing from within ourselves so it can blossom.

Nowadays, the corporate enquiries I receive are as likely to be for psychic development as they are stress management, or selling with confidence or presentation skills. Successful business people are those who follow their instincts, gut feelings, heart, first reaction, etc., in their work and trust they are right when they take action while others may shake their heads in disbelief. Nice parents are those who trust instinctively how to help their children grow and develop confidence and manners. They don't hit them to teach them; they explain things calmly and show what is expected.

A perfect explanation of this is given by Cesar Milan, the Dog Whisperer, who says that we are all just energy; therefore, that is the only thing that dogs react and respond to, as they live 'in the now'. For them, energy is all that there is; they don't mull over their life or worry about what is going to happen. He insists that we must put out calm, assertive energy to elicit the desired response from the dog and for the dog to be comfortable.

If we are anxious or cross, the dog will respond to this. Likewise, if we're holding on to the dog's history of a sad or traumatic experience, that will make the dog confused. If you start to worry about how your dog will behave, you put out a nervous energy that confuses and agitates the animal. When I teach people about mind whispering it can be revelatory. As soon as we are 'clear' everything flows: for us and the dogs.

Using the techniques outlined in this book will help in all areas of your life: personally and professionally. You have probably already had intuitive moments, but maybe they were disregarded. Have you ever met someone who you instantly disliked but went against your judgment, only to find out later you were right to be concerned? Likewise, you have probably been drawn towards a person who seemed warm and approachable and they were exactly that. Have you ever said, 'I knew that would happen'? Or not been in the least bit surprised at an unusual event's outcome? These examples perfectly demonstrate that you already know a lot more than you 'know'.

This is your route for 'tuning in' to awaken or build the skills within your natural self. The subjects covered can be for self-use, if you are seeking to develop as a light-worker, to enhance the talents you are already using or if you wish to take over the world.

In a dictionary nutshell:

Psychic – of or relating to the soul or mind.
Intuition – the ability to understand something immediately, without the need for conscious reasoning.

Together we will remove the weird, the wacky and the woo-woo without losing the magic and charm available to you in your inner and outer world. You can live the psychic way by fine-tuning your intuition.

Be sincere; be brief; be seated.
Franklin D. Roosevelt

2

Once Upon a Time

Sometimes I've believed as many as six impossible things before breakfast.
Lewis Carroll, Alice in Wonderland

Once upon a time there was a little girl called Barbara. She lived in an ivory tower singing like an angel while the birds and little animals came in the house to talk to her. Life was blissful and – insert screeching skid noise – oh no, that wasn't me! Of course that was Snow White and actually my life was, is, more Alice in Wonderland. Plus, I can't sing.

Growing up, I spent a lot of time in the company of myself. Both my parents worked and as an only child when I wasn't with friends my time was with adults or alone. I loved my freedom as it gave me the opportunity to allow my imagination to run wild; usually this was good but occasionally, not so.

I didn't particularly like school, as I always seemed to be worrying that I was about to be told off. It was a valid fear, because there was always something better to do than learn the algorithm of custard amidst remembering the route from sheep to jumper that wool takes in Australia. Is it any wonder that I drifted off in those lessons? Actually, school is probably one of the first most noticeable times when we all drift off into a trance-like state. When I was about nine, I stayed over at a friend's house whose father was one half of a famous TV scriptwriting duo and their huge town house was the most amazing place ever. We played in the back of the Rolls Royce (like you do) and I was having the best fun until bedtime when her older brother, plus a few of his friends, joined us and proceeded to share ghost stories that, quite frankly, frightened me almost to death. I was too scared to go to the bathroom alone and began to wish I was somewhere else, anywhere else would have done.

Back home, terrified of everything including my own shadow, I experienced my first lesson in the law of attraction with ghosts, ghoulies and long-legged beasties being the order of the day. Everyone seemed to be talking about something spooky and I also started to become more aware of the mistiness around people that somehow gave me indications of the person's moods or if they weren't well. I had always seen this haze but just accepted it and assumed that everyone else did too.

When I told my mum that I thought a friend of hers was poorly because of the way the 'fuzzy bit' around him looked and he died shortly after it was very disturbing. I didn't want to be the harbinger of doom, what with all the lurking spooks, I was sure were watching me from the shadows, ready to make me jump at every turn. When I told my mum my fears she took me to see her lovely friend, who we called Mrs. P, who told fortunes and read palms. She didn't look at mine but she rested her hands on either side of my head and whispered that I was 'special' as my powers were already tuned in. Woe betide me if I didn't use them wisely. It felt like she had got into my head with her hot buzzing hands and it was as if I had pins and needles in my brain.

Wow! My thoughts? Daft old bat.

However, I was very excited at the thought of being like Samantha in *Bewitched*, but despite spending ages trying to twitch my nose, I never quite managed even with my efforts and hard wishing.

Regardless of my initial disdain I spent plenty of time at Mrs. P's home and while she and my mum nattered over copious pots of tea, I amused myself with what she referred to as her 'tools'.

These were tarot cards, runes, oils, crystals and an

assortment of paraphernalia that would be at home in any witch's cupboard. I didn't know what they were called or used for at the time, but I remember holding some of the cards (Tarot) and getting images forming in my head. On one occasion, she performed a ritual of swirling tea dregs in a cup and, after emptying away the liquid, tipped it upside down on the saucer. After lifting it she then asked me what I saw in the cup and when I smugly replied, 'Tea leaves', she told me to look into and beyond them. They looked like little clods of mud but strangely they took on shapes that seemed to mean something as I rattled off what appeared in my mind. At this she nodded and smiled knowingly.

When I was about thirteen, I realized that most people didn't see the glow or colored fuzzy bits around others in the same way as me. Or, if they did, no one mentioned it. It became apparent that that sort of thing wasn't talked about and so I 'tuned' out and stopped letting the images and thoughts about people float into my mind. I tried to become normal and behave in a conventional manner – whatever that means.

Life from then was pretty normal. Occasionally, I would 'know' things about people, although I didn't let on, but if I sensed that someone was poorly I would silently wish them better if that was what they wanted. One of the lessons from Mrs. P was that we mustn't inflict ourselves on others uninvited. We cannot and must not try to force healing on them if they don't want it. It took me many years to really understand this, as I thought that surely everyone would want to be healed or helped. But, none of us know what is best for anyone else. We only know about us. Even if we are sure we know and want to insist on passing our 'rightness' to those we perceive as in need, if our opinions aren't wanted we should keep them to ourselves.

Jump forward in time to the mid-eighties. I was a working mum and suffered a back injury at work. This left me quite disabled for many years, as I underwent various treatments and operations. The first operation had seemed partly successful but a couple of years later my back seized up and it became apparent that all wasn't well. I was readmitted to hospital while the new surgeon decided on a cunning plan and after a few days bed-rest the nurses helped me up to see if the resting had helped.

As we went along the corridor, I drifted into a slow-motion hazy world that began when I realized I couldn't actually feel my legs. As I looked down, it was apparent that I had wet myself but had no feeling or awareness, but in the next moment I was standing in front of a large group of people talking and laughing with them.

Then I was back on the bed with a lovely nurse stroking one hand and the surgeon holding the other. They told me I had passed out and I must have looked very confused wondering how I'd managed to have a dream about lecturing in such a short amount of time. The surgeon told me the previous operation had completely failed and another was to be done immediately. The hours that followed blurred in my mind until I came round after the operation more muddled than ever. I had spent more time lecturing and it continued in the post-anesthetic sleep of the days after. Questions were tossed about in my thoughts. Was I dreaming or imagining? The more I thought, though, the more it didn't seem like a dream as it was too 'real'. In one of them I was in a room with golf memorabilia talking to women, and in another I had my hands resting on someone's head.

However, at that time, there was no way on earth I would have contemplated lecturing and, anyway, what would I lecture on? I also found it confusing and odd that in some of my visions of lectures the people had their eyes closed.

While all this was happening I also began to see auras again and 'know' people's thoughts. I decided it was a pain and anesthetic related reaction and although I let the images slip from my mind they often drifted into my awareness and dreams.

After I had recovered, I was at a crossroads in my life and decided a new career was in order. I studied psychology and counseling, but neither particularly excited me enough to devote myself into developing a career of those modalities. One day I spotted a classified advert about hypnotherapy in *The Lady* magazine and felt drawn to it even though, to be perfectly honest, I didn't really know much about hypnosis, but my instincts were poking me in the direction of discovering more. The more I found out, the more I felt driven towards it and so decided to get qualified and open my own clinic.

My work seemed to naturally drift towards working with groups and in one of those sessions, while I was leading a guided meditation, I remembered the dream from when I was in hospital with me talking while everyone had their eyes shut. I had a moment of déjà vu that whooshed into my awareness with such force it felt like the air movement you get as the train approaches in the underground. Soon after having been invited to talk at a ladies' golf presentation I had another and realized that the dreams had been premonitions. Hence, why they felt more solid and real than regular dreams. I think in moments of trauma we can get glimpses of possible future events as a guide of what is coming or as a reassurance that all will be well. Unfortunately, we don't tend to know that at the time, but these 'dreams' are comforting and I believe that they help us to cope with whatever is happening.

As my hypnotherapy practice grew, the hidden abilities I'd tucked away all those years before started to push forwards again. I knew how my clients were feeling from the state of their chakras and auras. I also knew when people were lying or keeping information from me in our sessions, but as their therapist I had to respect their decision to do so. After all, I am not the truth fairy.

Some, actually most, of my clients would tell me their star-sign at our first meeting as if that was the reason or excuse for whatever was happening to them. They would say things such as, 'I can't stop smoking but then I am a Leo', or 'I'm quite distrusting because I analyse so much. That'll be the Virgo in me'. It was as if my clients sensed my abilities before I actually fully admitted them to myself.

When my youngest son, Martyn, was at primary school, I found myself agreeing to be the fortune-teller at the annual May Fayre. Due to unforeseen circumstances the soothsayer gypsy wasn't available so they roped me in at the last minute and, after all, I couldn't say no to the vicar.

My plan was to have a laugh and to share information by having a brief chat with my customers, during which they would mostly do-it-themselves, rather than the, 'You'll meet a tall dark stranger', type of mystical interlude. For this I would need some props and so I collected pebbles from the beach to make into runes. As I drew shapes onto the stones I remembered, by then the long dead, Mrs. P and was sure I could hear her knowing chuckle. I also designed posters to write out the traits of each star sign and drew a big hand with the meanings of the various lines.

On the day, after donning hoop earrings and a shawl, I climbed aboard my besom and swooped down the hill to settle in behind the veil – oh okay, tent flap – and waited, fully expecting to sit there for the duration without a single visitor. To my surprise, I had a queue for the whole afternoon and when I wandered off to watch the children maypole dancing, I practically had a riot. Those hot silver fifty pence pieces were burning holes in their hands, so keen were they to cross my palm.

As each fortune tellee entered my sanctum, I asked them to pick three runes that we then read about together from my notes. We talked about the astrological meanings of their star-sign and I looked at their hands to match the lines to my drawings. As I was able to read what was going on with them, I slipped in the occasional comment of what I detected. On that day it was all about playing and making a little money for the school, but by the end of the afternoon it was clear that people wanted more. The personal information and questions from those fete visitors was astounding.

This was quite a revelation to me, as it demonstrated that there was such a huge interest in all things 'out there'. Gradually, in the years that followed, as more people began asking me how their auras were looking or if their chakras needed balancing, I began to allow my authentic self to blossom. By that, I mean I allowed myself to share the abilities that I use and teach others to make the best of their talents and skills that are already present, as I do in my work and general day-to-day living.

It is my belief that we all have these abilities but they are tucked away, ignored or denied and often ridiculed by those who think they know better. Maybe you had similar experiences in your childhood as I did and you can remember filing away the knowledge for a rainy day.

Imagine now that day has arrived. Let's share and learn while, hopefully, having a bit of fun on the way.

3

Where's Your Head At?

Since everything is in our heads, we had better not lose them.
Coco Chanel

While recovering from my back injury and subsequent surgeries I used relaxation and focused mind techniques to manage pain and accelerate healing. I knew a bit about breathing from having babies (hold breath in until blue and scream profanities while forcing it out!) and how powerful our minds could be if we made use of our inner powers. With any pain or discomfort, the more we are able to relax the more comfort we feel. However, don't try telling that to a woman in the throes of labor or she'll probably kill you stone dead with a tongue-lashing!

When I started my training as a hypnotherapist I realized our powers were even stronger than I thought as I witnessed many amazing things. Seeing someone's chronic pain fade (literally by the change in their aura as well as the relief seen in their face) or a 3-5 pack a day puffer becoming a non-smoker is very humbling. I, myself, had a phobia of flying that had restricted my life for years until I watched it float away – never to trouble me again.

As if all this wasn't wonderful enough I also discovered that my intuition became finely tuned, which gave me a better sense of my life direction and the skills to help my clients through their life changes.

In a hypnotherapy session the trance state is shared with the client in a way that a good therapist will tune into them fully to work in perfect balance on a subconscious level.

Therefore, one of the first lessons when developing psychic

intuition is the art of inner peace. You will not be able to notice your instincts working if your mind is anxious or flying round the lights pumped with adrenaline. Imagine tuning in a radio and getting stuck between signals; you get a muddled mix of voices, music and static buzz. Nothing is clear and it is irritating. When we are buzzing we emit an internal cacophony in the form of over-thinking or niggles and worries. It becomes hard to rest and relax; so much so that at times it is difficult just to think or remember things. If you're stressed you can forget names or you may have even said, 'I'm so stressed I can't think straight', or 'Now what was I meant to be doing?' but all you get back is fizz (metaphorically of course). When you can enter a state of calm you are better able to tune into your feelings and surroundings.

Your psychic abilities and intuition are freed up and can develop more fully when you are able to use the right-hand side of your brain and not be stuck in the analysis of the left. Your left-brain hemisphere works with reason; you look at something and deduce what it is you are seeing with logic. Your right-brain hemisphere is responsible for your creativity and imagination. We can think of them as separate entities or complete in their own right. The left-hand side is usually referred to as the male, while the right is the feminine or the conscious and subconscious mind. If there is something we don't quite understand our mind can become very inventive and this is often the way phobias get strong because we over-imagine.

I tend to think of the brain and mind working harmoniously with the focus I require in any given moment in the exact place I need it. A good metaphor for the mind is to think of a theatre; the audience sees the finished production but is not privy to the hard work going on behind the scenes. The conscious mind is the bit on show and everything else that happens beneath the surface is hidden, backstage. There are some experts who insist that the conscious and subconscious do not exist and we are just 'mind', but for our purposes I think it is best to think of them as separate but working together.

If you were to squeeze a tube of toothpaste would you grab and scrunch (right-brain) or would you methodically start at the bottom and push out the exact amount (left)? What about if you are eating bread and a spread? Would you put the used butter knife into the jam and blob on any old amount (right) or use a clean one to deliver the exact portion (left)? Do you analyse most things that you experience, deliberating with yourself and spending time logically working through a particular course of action, or do you just trust your instincts so that if it feels right you let it happen?

When we are in 'left-brain mode' we think and behave logically, sequentially and methodically. We plan and analyze – sometimes to destruction. From this behavior we get the term 'analysis paralysis'. It can be so disabling that the person who constantly functions like this might end up unable to do anything or runs the risk of developing an obsessive-compulsive disorder. I have seen this happen a lot in my work with performers and sportspeople. Take golfers for instance; they replay their game in their mind over and over, often to the point of destruction, convincing themselves how useless they are and then when they next play they start at the point of being a failure and their game tends to become stressful. They make silly mistakes which in turn reconfirms the earlier thoughts. Likewise, performers can over-criticize and lose their self-belief very easily. If they mess up an audition through performance anxiety or get turned down for a role that they were sure belonged to them, they can easily slip into a downward negative spiral.

When we are in 'right-brain mode' we think and behave intuitively with feeling and imagination, going with our hearts but maybe not paying quite enough attention to the goal or logic. You may know people who seem to be away with the fairies most of the time, living in a fluffy world and too much of this type of thinking might mean losing touch with reality.

It is generally said that men are left-brain dominant and women right-brained. Or, pedantic male versus intuitive female. It might be, for example, that you logically know or understand something but your imagination creates another reality.

An interesting phenomenon is if you see something that doesn't make any sense in the context of what you know or everything else you can see or hear; you often won't realize it is there. For example, in the film *What the Bleep* it is stated that when Christopher Columbus approached land, the Native Americans didn't see the ships because they had never seen ships before; to them, they didn't exist. While some might label this as a myth, there is a perfect demonstration of this in action in the classic *YouTube* video called 'Test Your Awareness'. Please check it out when you get chance.

Similarly, if you are looking for something but your mind is busy or the object is in a different place than usual, you can't see it. This is called a negative hallucination. Close-up magic relies on us not noticing what is directly in front of us, because we are occupied in our thoughts while being distracted with something different to look at.

The opposite of this is over-imagining: usually by thinking yourself into a state of fear when there isn't enough information forthcoming. This can happen in those sleepy half-awake moments when disturbed in the night, convinced that there is someone in the room, only to reveal itself as a dressing gown when the light is put on. Also, being highly stressed can make rational thought difficult because the amount of effort required maintaining the stress ensures that clear thought becomes impossible.

Being constantly stressed uses up a lot of energy and brain-power, while tending to keep us in a left-brain mode unless we metaphorically explode when it becomes too much. This is the path to a nervous breakdown, so way before that happens it is important to remember that we need balance.

Tuning in your intuitive abilities begins by awakening the right-hand side of your brain to allow your creativity to flow. You will, apart from developing skills, allow your health to benefit enormously as stress is automatically reduced. In fact, regular meditation has been shown to lower blood pressure and to boost the immune system.

All you need to do then is meditate for a bit and release all your stresses to allow everything to blossom. But herein lays the challenge for many. Relaxing can be hard as it has become an abnormal state and we are mostly running about chasing our tails. Our language confirms this when we are on the school run, running for the bus or for president, run-ragged and so on. Meditation seems to belong to an elite group of crossed-legged devotees who have been ohm-ing and ah-ing for many years. This, of course, isn't true but I have heard that description more than once.

One of the difficulties is the belief that somehow the only way to measure success is to hit a nirvana moment the second you sit on your yogi stool with a mind full of emptiness. Whereas, in reality, your mind will most likely wander with thoughts popping in and falling from your head most of the time and the more you try to still yourself or stop them the more they will do their best to disturb you. Your experience will be personal to you and whatever happens is right for you.

I'd like to mention the difference and similarities between hypnosis and meditation and how, by blending the two, that most desirable state of peace will be yours. My son suggested mixing the words to come up with hypnotate or meditise.

When in a hypnotic state the mind is very focused: closing in, and when in a meditative state it is free: opening out.

Therefore; hypnosis = flowing in, and meditation = flowing out.

Brain waves

Developing the skill of hypnotic meditation ensures that your brain slows; in this state you will be at your creative peak.

The activity in our brains is measured in waves called Hertz (or pulses) in amount per second. There are:

Beta – 13 - 30 cycles per second. Busy, thinking, active.
Alpha – 7 - 13 cycles per second. Relaxation, meditation, creativity.
Theta – 4 - 7 cycles per second. Dreaming, meditation, ESP.
Delta – 1.5 - 4 cycles per second. Deep sleep below dream-level.

Throughout the day we are mostly in beta with dips into alpha. If we keep our brains buzzing all day it is often a struggle to sleep well at night, as we need to go through every level in order to get a nourishing slumber. If stressed, the starting-off point at bedtime is one of activity instead of one of calm in preparation to drift into a peaceful slumber.

We have many sayings and contradictions: not in a right mind if breaking the law or acting in an unusual manner, but in a right state if upset or traumatized. It might be that you are not in the right place mentally if you wish to try something new or you want to relax. Think for a minute about your state of mind. Is it one of inner calm or stress? Excitement or torpor? Balance or all-over-the-show?

There are two hypnotic-type states of mind that occur naturally pre- and post-sleep, namely the hypnagogic and hypnopompic. The first is in the twilight world, where you are just drifting off, and the second is that delicious time as you awaken. Many people have their brilliant ideas and eureka moments in the early hours when everything is resting and there aren't any intrusions on your brain. This is a time of highly tuned intuition when thoughts and energies flow freely.

However, this time of pleasure can be marred by stress when we awaken with thoughts whirring and internal chatter bombarding our senses. It is no wonder that this is called 'monkey brain'.

In my clinic and the classes I teach I have found that the relaxing bit is actually easy once we give ourselves permission to do so, but it is the maintenance of the relaxation that is a bit harder. However, with a little practise, it is attainable for everyone. Separating relaxation from sleep is one of the first steps, but often, if there is a lot of stress, the moment relaxation comes on sleep takes over through escape and relief.

Often, the comments from my clients after our first session are contradictory: 'I drifted off. I didn't hear a word you said'. Others say, 'I didn't sleep. I heard every word you said'. On further questioning, the ones who thought they had dozed off hadn't, and the ones who insisted they heard it all didn't.

Minds wander. It's what they do – nature of the beast and all that – but concentrating hard on preventing that happening can cause anxiety with even more wandering. It is a cycle that can be hard to break if you're not aware what is going on. Our mind needs action. Even during sleep the mind stays busy by creating stories to occupy those moments in the form of dreams. It really doesn't like to be told to stop its thinking.

Try now to not think for a few moments and then do the following: imagine a table, nothing else, just a table. I bet within seconds your table was in a room or being used. You might have had it laid with chairs around it waiting for those people who have just come to sit down for their meal. I just tried it, and on my table was one of those silver dishes where the lid is removed with a flourish. From that I drifted off to *Fawlty Towers* when Basil is collecting the duck and he beats the car with a tree branch when it breaks down. All this took about three seconds to slip all that way from my starting point.

Over the years, I began to think: why not use that mind

wandering ability in our favor? We can do this by flowing through, into and with the spaces or gaps between the moments of organized thought rather than battling with them. Your mind is then occupied and focused but in a peaceful, non-threatening, non-challenging way. When it then doesn't need to worry about being still, stillness is created. It is exactly the same process as when we tell ourselves that we can't have something, i.e. chocolate or cigarettes. That is all we think about. When we have something in abundance, without the fear of deprivation, the craving dissipates. As Gary said in the BBC comedy, *Men Behaving Badly*, 'When there's always biscuits in the tin, where's the fun in biscuits?'

Please remember that nothing is just something pretending.

The way forward from here is to use hypnotic meditation to relax with ease and allow your mind to rest so thoughts can be clear and receptive. Within a short time it will become natural and easy to replicate.

4

Hypnotic Meditation

All serious daring starts from within.
Joan Baez

When you meditate you 'are' and you open out.
When you are in hypnosis you 'are' and you focus in.
When you are in hypnotic meditation you just 'are'.
Meditation = flowing out – in the zone
Hypnosis = flowing in – in the zone
Hypnotic meditation = flowing – in the zone
By blending them you can enter the flow-zone.

Have you ever been mesmerized, maybe by music, a film, book or just people watching? The word comes from Franz Anton Mesmer: a cape-wearing showman who, in the late eighteenth century, believed people slipped into an altered state by way of what he called animal magnetism. He had named it animal magnetism and would host huge performances whereby he used iron rods in a wand-like way or had people hold the rods that were attached to huge containers. The whole extravaganza would cause many attendants to convulse or slip into catalepsy. Throughout the demonstration Mesmer would speak in hushed tones delivering suggestions for recovery or release from pain.

James Braid, a nineteenth century Scottish doctor, coined the word 'hypnosis' from abbreviating neuro-hypnotism, meaning sleep of the nerves. After he became fascinated by oriental meditation he reasoned that it was the same as a self-induced 'nervous sleep'; nerves sleeping rather than a state of shock and shutdown. He also saw, first-hand, a demonstration of mesmerism by the French man Charles Lafontaine. Braid recognized that it was possible to induce this state, sometimes called rapture, in oneself without the need to be mesmerized. Braid is known nowadays as the father of modern hypnotism for his work, research and use of suggestion treatments to help his patients.

The actual word 'hypnosis' is derived from Hypnos the Greek God of sleep who had the ability to bewitch people into 'sleep with eyes open', which is what we now refer to as trance.

Throughout history there has been a crossover of healing techniques, as the power of dreaming has long been known about. In Ancient Greece and Egypt, for example, sleep temples were built. It was believed that dreams were, and by many still are, the link to our soul, and that problems can be identified and healed through analysis and treatment. As dreams are created and played through subconsciously, hypnotic techniques have been regarded in much the same way with the only difference being wakefulness. During sleep, our mind is free to sort and file the events and happenings of the day or the past, and the slight awareness we have during this time is occupied by dreams. I think this is so we don't interfere by saying things, such as, 'Don't put that thought there', or 'I'd rather forget that; please put in the bin'. During trance-work (sometimes referred to as controlled daydreaming, waking sleep or creative visualization) the filing and organizing is done in a more systematic way.

Psychotherapy has traditionally been a long on-going process, as it was felt that everything should be analyzed and dissected to make sure the reasoning behind behavior or actions was understood. This was believed necessary to facilitate a cure or release. Nowadays, we are schooled in much quicker techniques that might include therapy during trance and rapid change techniques, such as EFT (Emotional Freedom Technique) or TFT (Thought Field Therapy). We know that problems can be resolved, in some cases, instantaneously when the time is right.

Self-hypnosis and meditation, as stand-alone tools, are widely used by many people for sport, stress management, child-birth, healing and change-work with an ever-growing number of people learning or using various hypnotic techniques as tools for self-improvement or to alleviate issues or difficulties.

Hypnotic meditation is something everyone can do, as the trance state is a natural occurrence that we all slip in and out of frequently throughout each day. Can you think of a time when you were in your car and, on arrival at your destination, realized that you had 'forgotten' parts of the journey? Have you ever been so completely absorbed in a book or a task that you became unaware of your surroundings? Have you ever totally lost yourself in lovemaking?

Think about how easy it is to become so deeply engrossed in your own thoughts that you don't notice what is happening or if someone is speaking to you.

Children first slip into trances when they suckle and then later while listening to stories or mesmerized by the TV. This continues in school during lessons and is very evident in university lecture halls as many of the students will appear asleep. I am not suggesting that some of them aren't asleep but several are in a concentrated mode (trance) of listening. There are many examples of everyday trances, so the experience of differing mind states is one that is familiar.

In formal hypnosis sessions the mind focus is usually accompanied by physical relaxation, during which time the conscious mind is occupied to allow access to the subconscious to deliver positive suggestions and to make changes using therapeutic techniques. When we use the techniques on ourselves, the relaxation part is a personal decision. For our purposes, the context is more about 'stilling', 'centering' and being 'at one with oneself'.

Positive thinking with awareness of being in the present moment is a good habit to have, as the subconscious mind is always very obliging – giving us exactly what we think about. Have you ever taken a pretend sick-day only to get ill?

The saying, 'Be careful what you wish for', is one worth remembering. When I was about nine years old I pretended to be ill to get a day off school when we were having a test. I felt so proud and clever for fooling my parents. About a month later, we were going on a school trip to London Zoo and I was so excited I thought I would burst. On the day of the visit I awoke with a raging temperature and couldn't go. I was devastated at the unfairness of it and when the doctor said I had scarlatina and would be off school for a week I burst into tears at the meanness of it all. In my feverish state, I confessed that I had fibbed before and asked if that was why I was now ill. The doctor laughingly admonished me and said it is possible to imagine ourselves poorly by pretending, and I vowed to never again feign illness. This was perhaps my first lesson in karmic repercussions. It might be that the 'wish' turned into a self-fulfilling prophecy and I now know we are and become exactly what we think: meaning that whatever we think about tends to happen. Whatever and wherever you are 'at' in your life now is the life created by your thoughts, so if you don't like it you can begin to change it.

People often, even if they are miserable in their life or the circumstances they are in, do nothing about it because they are comfortable with the familiarity. I have had people describe lives of misery and they end by saying, 'That's how it is though'. They might be in a relationship without any pleasure but stick with it, because 'they know where they are' and 'better the devil you know'. Also, they might believe or think that there is nothing they can do as 'life' is beyond their control and they are carted along in everyday living without a say in the matter.

I think of it as the trance of living but when we notice what is happening – if we don't like things or are not happy with something – changes can be made. The mind states we then slip into are the ones that allow us to reach fulfillment and happiness.

We are all in various levels of wakefulness, tiredness or focus depending on what we are doing at any given moment. As these changes happen naturally we need to notice how we, as individuals, experience variations in consciousness.

Think of what is occurring right now. How are your levels of concentration and how are you feeling? Are you absorbed in reading this or is your mind elsewhere so that you can't quite remember what you have just read? Did you go back and re-read to check and now you can't remember again?

How do you feel when you are cross, calm, happy, peaceful or sleepy? So often we just float through each day by just getting on with it and not paying attention to anything that happens within ourselves. You will soon find that as your awareness of differing states becomes recognizable it is then easier to induce a useful and workable state of hypnotic relaxation.

We automatically drift into a trance-like state if we do anything repetitive or boring. If we concentrate, fix our attention or bombard ourselves with too much information, away we go – shut down, chill out, wander-off, daydream! At the gym, having repetitive bass music playing lulls those exercising into a dream-like daze where they can tread the mill for longer than if they were actually thinking about what they were doing. Reading is another good example of inducing a natural trance. I often find myself completely absorbed in a book to the point that when I stop reading it takes a while to 'come back' to full reality. By practicing self-hypnosis we can get so good at it that just a few seconds of focus is all we need – this is assuming that there are no mental or psychological blocks hindering us. When in hypnosis the mind is receptive to sugges-tions, affirmation and ideas, so introducing self-hypnosis to your everyday routine can help enormously with everything: from stress management to healing, from living more psychically to boosting confidence, from phobia removal to giving birth smiling!

I think one of the most important lessons is to know what hypnosis actually is, and in particular what it isn't, as the first step towards using it as a tool. I am often asked how it feels to 'go under', as people think they will sink under the radar of waking consciousness but are unsure where they are slipping to or might end up. It is easier then to think of it as something you enter or go into rather than 'under'. Hypnosis and meditation are not sleep and you will not become a zombie in a deep coma-like state without your wherewithal ready to be ordered to obey commands or give away personal information. Even though the appearance of someone deeply relaxed or in a trance has lead many to the belief that those in hypnosis or meditating are sleeping or unaware of what is going on around them, this is not so. So many times, despite explaining this, I have clients who still think they will be asleep and are amazed when they remain awake; it shows how deep our programming and expectations run.

The familiarity of a trance state leads some to the conclusion that they 'can't do it' or that it doesn't 'work'. It is important to just go with the flow and enjoy whatever happens because however you experience it, it will be the perfect way for you.

As you learn self-hypnosis your inner and outer awareness develops to strengthen the awareness of your mind/body connection. This knowledge will begin to naturally extend beyond your physical body to enable you to receive intuitive messages and ideas.

See, Hear, Feel
Many people call relaxation exercises 'creative visualization'. However, not everybody visualizes in the same way. It is useful to be aware of how your thought processes work so that you can create successful hypnotic techniques that are relevant to you.

Think for a moment about the front of your home. Suppose I asked you to describe it to me. What would you say?

I'll describe mine: The building is red brick with wooden-framed windows and the front door is a stable design with a solid bottom. I can 'see' an image of it in my mind.

However, if I asked my daughter the same question she would describe it in the same way but she doesn't 'see' a picture in her head. She would say she thinks it. Other people describe places, objects and people by how they feel. A few 'hear' their thoughts and/or talk to themselves.

Do you now know how you think?

If you see images and pictures in your head or mind's eye and you say things like, 'I can't picture that myself', or 'I see what you mean', you are visual.

If you talk to yourself in your head and you say things like, 'I hear you'. or 'Do you hear what I'm saying?' you are auditory.

If you operate and seek representations in feelings and you say things like, 'I feel I want to', or 'That really doesn't feel right to me', you are kinesthetic.

It is no good telling someone who is very auditory to picture something. They need to utilise their self-talk in order to achieve their goals. However, I think that everyone who has sight has the ability to see in their imagination, but because they might not see it as a clear real image they dismiss it. The mental imagery might just be a color awareness or a sensation of shape, size or texture and that is fine. Whether you do or don't see pictures in your head doesn't really matter as long as you are aware of what is expected of you. If I ask you to imagine a tree you might not need to create a picture perfect image of one and you don't need to as just the thought will do; plus, I'm sure you know what a tree looks like. Another way to check for yourself how you 'think' is to imagine a jar of pickled onions. Are you seeing the jar with the onions in it, smelling the tangy vinegar, imagining the taste, or is your mouth watering?

For our purposes I will use the word 'imagine' and you can do whatever you would usually do when you think and use your imagination. Can you imagine doing that? If you can't then just pretend.

And however you think and imagine: it is right.

Relaxing into Hypnotic Meditation

There is a full script for the color/number meditation at the end of this chapter, but first try out the following during the day, preferably sitting, not lying down.

If you always fall asleep you can practise relaxing when you are feeling awake. Although the use of positive suggestions and powerful affirmations just as you drop off to sleep is a good thing, it is beneficial to be able to use hypnotic techniques without always falling asleep.

Complete muscle relaxation is a good place to start but not always necessary because in reality you do not have to be deeply relaxed in order to slip into a trance. But, for the purpose of this, because it's nice and because it is good for your health and well-being, we'll begin with relaxation. Some people prefer to record instructions, so if you like that idea have a go and do whatever works best for you.

Make yourself comfortable and gently slow your breathing. Focus your mind on each part of your body, beginning with your feet and working upwards. Think about each muscle relaxing. Imagine you are breathing calm peaceful relaxation into every part of you. If you are very stressed or you find this difficult just pretend you are relaxing and think of words like soft, dreamy, melt, soothed.

While this is happening silently, to yourself, repeat, one, two, three, one, two, three, one, two, three until the numbers fall from your mind, you lose count or until you can no longer be bothered.

Really feel relaxation spreading through your whole being.

Pay particular attention to areas where you might experience stress: your neck, head, shoulders and tummy. Concentrate on relaxing those places where you feel any anxieties.

Imagine that you are breathing tensions away.

You may find that you are now becoming a little detached; enjoy whatever you experience.

Deepening

The next stage is a deepening. Some people are content to feel a light relaxation while others prefer to go a little deeper. It is better to try out a few ways to discover which you prefer. Think about what you would associate with going down or floating up into a deeply relaxed state.

Here a few ideas:

Going down steps.

Counting from one to ten where you have ten as deeply relaxed.

Counting as you imagine going down steps.

Imagining or thinking about watching something floating down, i.e. a leaf or feather.

Repeating words or phrases, i.e. deeper and deeper or calm and relaxed.

Saying a particular word to yourself as you breathe out, i.e. calm.

Contradictory words and thoughts work well – floating while sinking down or light as a feather, heavy as stone.

When you are at a happy level, create a special place in your mind. It can be somewhere that you know or you can invent a place.

If you are still counting you may now stop.

Make your special place as real as you can and really create a feeling of calmness and inner peace. Regard this as a place that you can visit in your mind at any time. When you are there all is well and you feel relaxed, calm and happy.

Scan yourself to check there are no little bits of tension. If you find any, breathe them away. Check that you are so deeply relaxed that apart from an emergency (at which point you would be immediately awake and alert) you can't be bothered to move because you feel so limp and lazily cozy comfy.

Using Suggestions

While you are in your hypnotic state you may want to use some suggestions or affirmations and yet again you have choices. You do not need to proceed to this if your purpose is just about the relaxation.

You will have determined if you have a particular need before you started, i.e. not smoking, playing a sport better, improving self-confidence or something else.

You can say your instructions or goals to yourself or you can imagine yourself as you would like to be.

Examples:

I am happy as a non-smoker.

My tennis is superb.

I can feel my confidence growing.

Or:

Imagine yourself in situations without cigarettes, hitting an ace, or having complete confidence in any situation.

You might try writing a list of sentences that denote your need and creating an image or symbol that represents them before your session and then when you are in trance just think of that image or symbol. Your subconscious will do the rest.

Be specific about what you want so that your subconscious mind can create a template to work towards and think of how it will be when you have achieved your desires.

Our minds work in the now, but will seek the most familiar inner instruction to activate actions or the ones with emotional attachment. Therefore, it is best to act 'as if' in your suggestions, thoughts, ideas and affirmations. If you have no particular needs just enjoy yourself and feel happy and healthy in mind and body.

When you are ready to be fully alert you can 'wake up' or you can count from five back down to one, telling yourself that you will be fully awake at the count of one.

You could set an alarm to alert you that it is time to end your session or you could have someone else let you know.

Four Stage Method to Calm Breathing

The following method makes use of color. You probably know the colors of a rainbow but if you don't, they are red, orange, yellow, green, blue, indigo and violet. I learnt them by remembering the first letters of each word in the phrase, '**R**ichard **of** **Y**ork **g**rew **b**lossoms **in** **v**ain'.

Try and give yourself eight to twelve minutes the first few times you practise stage one. As the stages after become easier, it will take you no time at all to sink down; it will become almost instantaneous.

Stage One

Make yourself comfortable and ensure you are warm enough and unlikely to be disturbed. Take a couple of calming breaths and close your eyes so you can use your imagination without any visual interference. Focus your mind on the color red. Notice any images or feelings associated with red and just acknowledge their presence. You might like to play about with the color. Think of how you might feel if you breathed it in and out. How would a room decorated in it be?

When you feel the time is right, let the red become orange

and repeat the whole process. Again, when ready, let it become yellow and then continue through the colors.

When you finish just imagine you are bathed in all the colors and become aware of which you associate with calm and inner peace. It might be that you prefer a blend of colors or that you make one up and if so that is fine.

Stage Two

Either continue straight after or make this a separate exercise.

You are going to focus your mind on the numbers, one through to seven. Each number is a color.

Because you have thought of the associations with each color you can now just have them as numbers. If this is too hard repeat Stage One a few times.

The idea is to get a rhythm of the numbers with the colors, thus:

Think of the number one and have it colored red. It might be a drawing, a solid block, a hologram or any other way you choose to create in your imagination the number one colored red.

Think about it for a few moments and then let it fade, spin or float away to be replaced by an orange colored two.

Repeat with the remaining numbers and colors so all in all you have,

One = red

Two = orange

Three = yellow

Four = green

Five = blue

Six = indigo

Seven = violet

When you reach the violet/seven, imagine the color softening and becoming paler and paler until it is almost white. Be bathed in the soft light or sensation of the color.

Just be for a little while.

Repeat Stage Two a few times until the colors are integrated with the numbers.

Stage Three

Without too much thought, count from one to seven and notice if you think of the colored numbers or picture the numbers associated with their colors in your mind.

If you don't or can't, just repeat Stage Two until you can.

Stage Four

Imagine the numbers resting one on top of the other, with red at the bottom and violet at the top. As you breathe in, take your mind (or if you picture the numbers, draw your eyes up) from one up to seven. As you breathe out go the opposite way. So, on the in-breath you go up and on the out-breath you go down.

The rhythm is in time with your breathing. Keep the pace of your breathing regular but the very nature of relaxing in this way will probably slow or deepen each breath.

You may notice that as you breathe out the pale violet is drawn down and gets paler as it passes through the numbers, which has the affect of bathing you in calm. Let that happen; let that violet fade and soften as you relax more and more.

Breathe this way a few times until you become aware of feeling calm.

I recommend you practise until you are comfortable all the way to Stage Four and then repeat it daily and before any of the exercises, rituals or techniques that will come later.

From now on, if I say calm breathing you will know what I mean.

After any meditation or psychic exercise please do something grounding. It can be a task like making a cup of tea, rubbing your feet on the floor or imagining roots stretching down your spine and legs and burying themselves in the earth.

Protection

Before we continue, it might be a good time to talk about protection. Some people are very negative and they act like psychic leeches draining others of their positivity and energy. You might know people like that. You dread asking them how they are for fear of them telling you. If you work with healing energies, part of helping someone else to feel better is to assist in their dumping of negative energy. This debris is certainly not something you want to gather up.

When I first started working as a therapist, I was told the importance of protection but I had to learn the hard way. I was sure I wouldn't take on board someone else's rubbish. Why would I do that? No, really, why? After about the fifth nightmare and being convinced that I had the same problems – only worse – as all my clients, I thought there might be something in it. After all, how many phobias and issues can one girl have?

Many psychics imagine that a protective white light surrounds them. One therapist I knew imagined putting on a silver space suit every morning. Some use mirrors to deflect negativity away from them and others create a bubble around themselves.

Over the years I have used all of these and I now have an automatic response that shoots up like the protective glass shield in building societies and garages.

Mine actually went off recently at a workshop before I had consciously registered a psychic vampire in my presence. For a moment I thought I might be overreacting, but yet again it was right.

Imagine you have a form of protection that allows positivity to flow in but deflects all negativity back. Whatever is going on in your life this will automatically make you feel more balanced and secure. If you feel someone is draining your energy, gently rest your hand on the area of your solar plexus, located between your navel and sternum, and this will stop it. (There is a protection meditation in the extra scripts.)

The purpose of practicing hypnotic mediation is that it becomes so easy and normal that it is accessible instantaneously. Despite good intentions, though, it is possible that you might find yourself stressed in particular situations. A quick tip to change that is to use the ABC method:

A = acknowledge whatever is happening – by being aware, any issues or difficulties immediately become smaller and less threatening.

B = breathe – stress can alter breathing patterns. This heightens anxiety. Make sure you breathe out fully.

C = calm – A+B = C.

Stress causes breath-holding or rapid breathing that can lead to hyper-ventilating and panic attacks. It rapidly dissipates as breathing becomes regular and then slower. The very act of breathing out fully creates calmness. Try it now and you will notice.

Script for Stage One

Make yourself comfortable and ensure you are warm enough and unlikely to be disturbed. Take a couple of calming breaths and close your eyes so you can use your imagination without any visual interference. Do everything slowly...

Focus your mind on the color red. Notice any images or feelings associated with red and just acknowledge their presence. You might like to play about with the color. Think of how you might feel if you breathed it in and out. How would a room decorated in it be?

Just be in that color or a while until you feel it is time to let it become orange.

Now, focus your mind on the color orange. Notice any images or feelings associated with orange and just acknowledge their presence. You might like to play about with the color. Think of how you might feel if you breathed it in and out. How would a room decorated in it be?

Just be in that color for a while, until you feel it is time to let it become yellow.

Now, focus your mind on the color yellow. Notice any images or feelings associated with yellow and just acknowledge their presence. You might like to play about with the color. Think of how you might feel if you breathed it in and out. How would a room decorated in it be?

Just be in that color for a while until you feel it is time to let it become green.

Now, focus your mind on the color green. Notice any images or feelings associated with green and just acknowledge their presence. You might like to play about with the color. Think of how you might feel if you breathed it in and out. How would a room decorated in it be?

Just be in that color for a while, until you feel it is time to let it become blue.

Now, focus your mind on the color blue. Notice any images or feelings associated with blue and just acknowledge their presence. You might like to play about with the color. Think of how you might feel if you breathed it in and out. How would a room decorated in it be?

Just be in that color for a while, until you feel it is time to let it become indigo.

Now, focus your mind on the color indigo. Notice any images or feelings associated with indigo and just acknowledge their presence. You might like to play about with the color. Think of how you might feel if you breathed it in and out. How would a room decorated in it be?

Just be in that color for a while, until you feel it is time to let it become violet.

Now, focus your mind on the color violet. Notice any images or feelings associated with violet and just acknowledge their presence. You might like to play about with the color. Think of how you might feel if you breathed it in and out. How would a room decorated in it be?

Allow the violet to become pale and soften all around you. You do not need to do anything; just be in the color or colors that are calming and relaxing for you.

When you are ready, gently awaken, maybe by counting back from seven to one and have a good stretch as you open your eyes.

End by grounding yourself.

5

Pendulum Time

The most effective way to do it, is to do it.
Amelia Earhart

Dowsing has been used for a very long time. There are cave drawings of dowsers in action and evidence that the Egyptians were skilled in the art 4000 years ago. Known also as divining or water witching, drilling and mining companies use it to locate their booty. Builders often get out their rods or bob to check for pipes or wires before drilling or they might also dowse for a water source.

One day, in the next village to me, the road needed digging up. The diggers and plant were poised ready for action patiently waiting for the dowser to tell them where to start digging. Despite the huge amounts of technology it is still often best to just call the diviner.

More recently, dowsing has become associated with health, as it can indicate changes or holes in our natural energy field (our aura), and can then show us when healing has occurred.

For our intention, we will use pendulums, but of course you are welcome to use hazel twigs or even bent coat hangers, as they will all do the job.

Pendulums can be as elaborate or as simple as you prefer. You can buy stones or crystals already attached to chain or cord; you may use a necklace with a ring, or even a small stone attached to a piece of string.

The pendulum itself is not a healing tool – you are. It amplifies the subtle movements in your body's energy to give a visual expression on what is occurring. If you send out the intention to heal, it is that that the pendulum detects and shows.

When you first get or make your pendulum, sit in a quiet meditative state for a few minutes and take calm breaths while holding it comfortably in your hands. There is no need to rush this; take your time to begin the tuning and bonding process. Often, in my workshops, attendants name theirs or get an impression of what the pendulum wishes to be called. It is a personal choice but you may find yourself very attached to it.

Chevreul's Pendulum

In 1833, the chemist, Michel-Eugene Chevreul, investigated the properties of pendulums and believed it possible to explain the responses in a scientific way. In so doing, he removed the occult theories that had previously prevailed. His belief was that the pendulum's reaction was a very technical term known as 'as if'. Excuse my quip, but we know that if we think or act 'as if' then that is what happens, and he realized that was what was happening. If you act confident and self-assured your mind cannot tell if it is real or imagined and so you become that person. If you think of something scary, before you know it you will feel frightened. Think of some delicious food – maybe your favorite meal – and I guarantee that within a short amount of time you'll feel hungry.

You might like to try out the following experiment:

Draw a circle with two crossed lines going through it.

Hold your pendulum in your dominant hand at the point of the cross and imagine it swinging along the up-down line. If nothing happens draw your eyes back and forth along the line. After a while the pendulum will begin to swing along the line.

Make it still again by gently resting it on the cross in the centre and repeat going across the other line. As before, if it is slow to respond, draw your eyes along the line.

Repeat the procedure now imagining it swinging around the circle first one way and then the other.

Do this a few times until you feel in tune with your pendulum. It reacts to you, your thoughts, desires and your personal subtle subconscious movements. If it doesn't move at all, gently start it off a few times and you will find it begins to do it itself. Keep it as yours, try not to share, but if you really must it is important to cleanse it by holding it under running water. Actually, cleanse it frequently regardless, especially if you carry out healing or clearing procedures.

The next step is to ask the pendulum to show you which way is yes and which is no. For some people it might hang still for one of the answers or it might vibrate, bounce or jiggle. I can't think of a better word to describe this and if yours does so you will understand exactly what I mean. I have just remembered in one class when someone's bounced straight up and down for a yes; it was like it was nodding.

To discover your pendulum's movements, either out loud or in your head, say, 'Please show me the yes motion'. Then repeat with, 'Please show me the no motion'. If it doesn't happen immediately be patient and repeat the earlier exercise.

Try asking a question that you know the answer to and see if it responds correctly. If it doesn't, check you have your yes and no the right way round. If it is still incorrect, give it a rinse and start again.

All the while you do this, you can hold it over your piece of paper or hover it over your other hand, your lap or just in the air. It is important to find the ways that work best for you. In my salons we've had so many variations that show there really isn't a right or wrong. I've seen pendulums daintily wiggle like an embarrassed schoolgirl and I've seen others swing so violently they could have an eye out.

Sometimes in our lives we need to make decisions or choices

that are hard and we might not know which is the best way or the right path to take. If you like, you can have a question and answer session with your pendulum by drawing an alphabet chart within a circle and allowing it to spell out the answers. Please be aware this can be a real eye-opener. You might be surprised, as you may well not get the answer you were expecting. Of course, you don't need to blindly follow the pendulum response, but you might open yourself up for discussion.

Before moving on let's discover how you tick. I'm not asking what makes you tick; this is about the how. I want you to know how you operate on a subconscious level and what is going on in your imaginative right brain.

What were your findings when you did the previous exercises on how you think? What do you mean, you didn't? Shall I wait while you go back?

If you don't want to, you might prefer trying the following: think about someone you know well, maybe even love. Focus your mind and thoughts on this person and be aware of how they look and what they might be doing. Imagine a conversation you've had or might have.

Did you see pictures in your head, feelings in your body or were you just thinking?

This is important because if I ask how it looks it might be that you 'see' with your mind's eye rather than seeing an actual image. If you are using your imagination, you are imaging (in your mind) but how we do that varies. However, whatever and however you do it, it is right for you.

A few years ago I did a whole course of therapy with a woman who only operated with her sense of smell. Yes, it was a challenge, but we like that.

I have worked with people who don't see auras with their eyes but they sense colors and 'know' how the person is feeling. Others, me included, can tune into someone's chakras without being physically present and be aware of their condition without ever seeing the person. It is an inner knowing or awareness.

It is fun to play games while you develop your dowsing skills. If you have someone with you, you can practise truth games. Have them pick a word from the dictionary and give you two meanings (one that is real and one that isn't), then have your pendulum decide. Or put a substance under one of a row of cups or bowls and try to discover which one it is under.

If you're feeling in the mood to begin testing your psychic abilities, ask someone to write down a number in between one and twenty and write it down and then fold the paper. Hold your pendulum over it and silently count until it swings the opposite way or until you get an affirmation of the number. One more is to have someone imagine a substance is under a bowl and you try to get it correct.

How can this be possible? Because, nothing is as it seems or doesn't. Nothing is solid as everything is made up of atoms vibrating at different rates. Dense things appear more solid but they are still full of gaps and space. Thoughts can become reality in the way that if you think about someone or something it or they will appear or contact you. Therefore, whatever the substance, you can tune into the vibrating energy that it emits and, as it will be different to the surrounding energy field, you will sense the change.

Light, in particular, is a definite trickster: is it a wave is it a particle? It can be either/or depending on the observer. It is pure witchcraft. If something as clear as light can change (ha ha get it?) its form, think of all the other possibilities.

We will return to our pendulums a little later.

6

Auras

The most beautiful thing we can experience is the mysterious. It is the source of all art and science.
Albert Einstein

As I previously mentioned, one of the first things that I was aware of as a child was auras. Some people will clearly see a haze or almost solid shape, while others sense auras emanating from anything living. I see a haze that sometimes does and sometimes doesn't have colors emanating from the chakras, but I am now able to turn it off so that I am not bombarded with information about people.

If our aura transmits our thoughts and emotions in an electro-magnetic energy field surrounding us then it follows that it is visible in varying degrees dependent on the light available to view it. Or does it? Decide at the end of the exercises.

Try first to feel your own etheric aura. This is the part of the aura closest to you. Begin with a little calm breathing and then put your hands together as if you are clapping and gently rub them together. Slide them into the position of prayer and very slowly separate them a few centimeters. Move them back and forth until you can feel a sensation of warmth or pressure. Repeat this hand movement again, but this time with your eyes closed and notice if it is easier if they are open or closed.

After this try feeling your aura on various parts of your body. If you are working with someone else, take turns with one having their eyes closed while the other rests their hand nearby until they feel the aura. One is sensing or feeling the other person's aura and the one with eyes shut is guessing whereabouts the other is 'touching'. Sometimes auras can feel tangible, like cotton wool or marshmallow. At first it might feel like a gentle breeze or buffeting to the person guessing where they are being 'touched'. Or, like I said before, it might just be a 'knowing' for the feeler and the one being felt.

Moving on now, try holding your hand in front of you, preferably in front of a pale colored wall and gaze at it. Just gaze or stare until you lose focus and it becomes as if you are looking straight through your hand and after a while the edges will soften. If you can do 'magic eye' pictures you will probably find this easy. If you can't do them easily this exercise will help you spot the hidden pictures tantalizingly just out of sight. Soon you will be aware of a haze surrounding your hand. It might be fleeting or only in one small area, but allow yourself to see or sense it without forcing it and without getting cross if you can't do so immediately.

Don't do anything else for a moment; just let it happen. If you aren't sure if you're managing, you can also try gazing at your hand in the same way for a minute or so and then close your eyes. You will have the aura of your hand imprinted on your retina. It won't be there long, but you should be able to see it.

Now try the following: put your hands in front of you as if going to pray, but leaving a gap between them, and wait until you see the aura. Very slowly, move your pointer fingers towards each other until they are almost but not quite touching. What do you see?

The same procedure will enable you to begin to see auras around people. Choose your subject, a friend is best or just someone who is happy for you to look at them for a while; please try not to get caught staring at strangers! No, really, even if you look at the back of their heads thinking they won't know, they will and you'll look like a mad stalker. Since the late 80s, the biologist, Rupert Sheldrake, has studied and written at length about 'the sense of being stared at'. We've all done it: stared at someone only for them to suddenly look back and make eye contact. If it is someone we're attracted to this is usually followed by a blush and a rapid change of eye direction with an almost irresistible urge to look straight back to see if they're still looking.

Okay, back to the experiment. Do the same as before: take a few calming breaths and fix your eyes at the top and slightly left of your subject's head, preferably with them in front of a pale colored wall so it will be easier to see. Let your eyes lose focus and soon you will see or sense their aura.

Some people are surprised that auras aren't static. They sometimes look wispy, almost like smoke; the edges move and occasionally you might see holes or gaps that can show illness or debris from mental or emotional difficulties. They can look a little like a heat haze that you see on runways, only smaller and more condensed.

For now, this is all you need to practise. Make sure you are comfortable sensing your own and other peoples' auras without acting like an excited puppy or squealing with delight if you are in public, as you start to see them more and more. This is especially important if you spot an anomaly. Please do not rush up to anyone saying something like, 'Do you know your aura has a hole in it?' – or anything else you might have spotted. You are not a walking diagnostician and you have learnt not to inflict yourself unwanted onto randoms.

When you first saw yours or another person's aura did you see a single or a mix of colors? For some people, colors seem to emanate or are associated with the chakras that we will discuss in the next chapter. With others, the whole aura may be one color or a dominant one that relates to how the person is doing or what they might be feeling.

If you can see or sense colors, here is an introduction to the meanings:

White: divinity and life energy – integrated mind, body and spirit.

Purple/lilac/violet: spirituality – open and receptive to all.

Indigo: psychic and intuitive abilities – third eye open or opening.

Blue: balance and ability – 'speak' to share or to protect others.

Green: balanced in giving and receiving love – strong heart, natural healer.

Yellow: strength, balance – energetic and nice to be near.

Orange: uplifting and inspiring – compassionate and caring.

Red: materialistic – strong balance of being grounded in reality.

Brown: unsettled, materialistic – negative thoughts.

Gray: dark or depressing thoughts – maybe split personality.

Of course, please take this as a guide only. Your own interpretations will be the ones that matter. Also, each color has various shades with differing meanings and the easiest way while learning is to remember that the brighter and clearer the color the more positive the emotional or physical state. Dirty, mucky or dull indicates congestion, self-doubts or illness.

In religious paintings, auras are depicted as halos, usually as white or wispy floating about above the head of person, saint or disciple. Sometimes, a glow is painted all around the revered to show pureness or holiness.

One more point I must make, though, is that some people never see colors in auras, even if they are very gifted or have spent years trying.

Take a rest now before we move on. Please do something grounding.

7

Chakras

Life is like an ever-shifting kaleidoscope – a slight change, and all patterns alter.
Sharon Salzberg

When I spoke earlier about the colored splodges around people that I first saw when I was young I was referring to the colors emanating from their chakras. Although I didn't have the knowledge as to the whys and wherefores, I sensed it all meant something and my interpretations were delivered purely by instinct.

What an interesting word that is, and while we are developing this natural ability we are learning to trust ourselves more by noticing the subtle changes and fluctuations in energies. This is often happening on a quantum level, but we respond to it as if it is a full-on visual, auditory and kinesthetic experience.

Chakra is the Sanskrit (classical language of India) word for wheel and you might think of them as cone-like vortexes that open to and into our body, mind and spirit. Through them our life energy flows. They offer a clear indication of how we are feeling and functioning on all levels of our being; when they are balanced we are healthy with a good feeling of well-being. Although there are many on our bodies and extending above us, we will concentrate on the main seven that stretch down from our crown.

Chakras spin alternately clockwise and anti-clockwise, but for our purposes we need to ensure they are opening and closing in alignment and at the appropriate times for our health: physical, mental, emotional and spiritual.

I imagine them like flood barriers in that it is important to allow all to flow, but not to let too much undesirable debris enter. You certainly don't want a backwash situation, as that could get messy. It is also not good to have closed chakras; as while nothing can get in, likewise nothing can flow away. They must be able to breathe and they need to be able to work in harmony with each other and with you and your environment.

We will begin with our own before thinking about helping other people. My favorite metaphor for assisting in the welfare of anyone else is that if the oxygen masks come down on the plane we must put our own on first before aiding anyone else. If your energies are all over the show, it would not be good to pass on that rubbish to others, and if you are running below par it would be best if you heal and balance yourself before anything or anyone else.

You probably instinctively know if your chakras are out of kilter: by feeling off balance, confused, muddled, out of tune, out of whack, blocked, congested, or, and this is one my favorite words, discombobulated.

One little blockage or dullness can cause any of those feelings or behaviors, and without resolution or relief those symptoms may worsen and lead to physical ailments.

You have probably heard of the term 'holding patterns'. This is when stress and anxieties sit in our body from the build up of an emotional attachment. Irritable Bowel Syndrome, IBS is often a stress reaction, as are some migraines and several other conditions. Sometimes, we hurt in the same places each time we are sad or upset and this is where we 'hold' the emotion. The Ancient Egyptians believed we thought with our heart, as this is often the place where we feel pain when emotionally upset or unstable. Some people refer to the heart as the emotional, the other or the second brain.

When we are unbalanced we may tend to have repetitive conditions, such as cluster headaches, upset tummies, fear of change, sore throats and/or nervous anxiety. The unwanted emotional, mental or physical clutter can build up slowly over many years or even lifetimes and it is best to clear our own before we can be any help to others. We will be clearing past-life debris later.

When you know if you have any holding patterns and where they are located you will have an understanding of what is happening in your own chakra system.

Also, knowing the chakra colors can help you diagnose any actual or potential problems and then move on to healing if necessary.

Again, I should explain that some people never see any colors, however hard they try. It might be the trying that stops it happening. But, it is more about the interpretation than the visual aspects of this, as with aura viewing. It may also be that it isn't necessarily a visual experience, but more about other senses coming into play.

As with everything, we are seeking balance, as too much of one color shows an overly active chakra. For example, someone looking or feeling blue might be down in the mouth, possibly miserable through unexpressed emotion or things left unsaid. Green with envy, well, there's that heart feeling again.

Thinking about where you feel emotional responses to people or situations will give you a good indication of possible areas to check. This doesn't always mean there is a problem and we mustn't assume that we all have something wrong somewhere. Some of us are balanced and clear thinking almost all of the time.

As part of your health and well-being routine, ensuring your chakras work at their optimum boosts your immune system and helps you to heal from any conditions you might already have.

Try the following:

Relax with calm breathing and gaze at yourself in a mirror. It is best to do this to yourself because when you look at other people their colors are filtered through yours. If you don't like mirrors, imagine yourself standing against the wall. However strange this may seem, it will work the same. It really does! You are not expecting to see your reflection on the wall; you are thinking of yourself by it. Gaze at each chakra in turn, allowing your eyes to soften in focus and become aware of any colors you see or sense. Are they bright, clear, mucky, dark, faded or patchy? When you have an idea of how they are, refer back to the holding patterns and it will tie in beautifully.

Okay, Maestro, from the bottom:

1. Red – This is the root or base chakra and is in between your bottom and your sexy bits. It is responsible for being grounded and stable. It relates to legs, feet, base of spine, bones and adrenal glands. From here, we show our levels of motivation, self-confidence and passion.

   Blockages or unbalanced signs are: instability (literally and metaphorically), feeling insecure, constipation, arthritis, spinal tensions or knee problems.

2. Orange – This is the sacral chakra and is in the centre of your abdomen. It is responsible for creativity and joy. It relates to the reproductive system, skin, bladder, lower intestine, spleen and gonads. From here, we show our self-respect and oomph.

   Blockages or unbalanced signs are: jealousy, negative emotions, sexual problems or bladder difficulties.

3. Yellow – This is solar plexus chakra and is in the centre of your being. It is responsible for cheerfulness and clarity. It relates to the stomach, liver, digestion, nerves, muscles, gall bladder and pancreas. From here, we show our energy levels and focus.

   Blockages or unbalanced signs are: fear, lack of confidence, perfectionism drive, ulcers or digestive disorders.

4. Green – This is the heart chakra and is level with your heart. It is responsible for harmony and peace. It relates to the heart itself, circulation, lungs, chest, blood and thymus gland. From here, we show our self-love and abundance levels.

   Blockages or unbalanced signs are: being over-emotional, giving or receiving affection difficulties, critical, heart problems or high blood pressure.

5. Blue – This is the throat chakra and is in the base of the throat. It is responsible for honesty and self-expression. It relates to throat, neck, lungs, ears and thyroid gland. From here, we show our honesty through our communication.

   Blockages or unbalanced signs are: communication issues, thyroid problems, ear, neck or throat problems.

6. Indigo – This is the third eye chakra and is in the centre of your brow. It is responsible for vision and protection. It relates to the left eye, nose, nervous system, lower brain, ESP and pituitary gland. From here, we show our wisdom and understanding.

   Blockages or unbalanced signs are: being overly cynical, fearful, lacking concentration, feeling detached, headaches, eye problems, vivid or unpleasant dreams.

7. Violet – This is the crown chakra and it is at the top of your head. It is responsible for clarity and pureness. It relates to the right eye, upper brain, nervous system and pineal gland. From here, we show our universal energy and inspiration.

   Blockages or unbalanced signs are: confusion, depression, low enthusiasm or inspiration, migraines or forgetfulness.

This is a nutshell at a glance guide:

RED – Base – grounding, stability, stamina, motivation, self-confidence, purpose, passion, excitement.

ORANGE – Sacral – joy, self-respect, release of negativity, creativity, cheer, happiness.

YELLOW – Solar Plexus – cleansing, cheer, happiness, upliftment, ego, will, energy, focus, enthusiasm, self-worth.

GREEN – Heart – balance, harmony, peace, abundance, self-love, emotional release, growth/new beginnings.

BLUE – Throat – release of physical tension, communication, peace, healing, honesty, calming, cleansing, self-expression.

INDIGO/PURPLE – Brow – wisdom, protection, vision, responsibility, understanding, seeking, power.

VIOLET/WHITE – Crown – clarity, cleansing, clearing negativity, universal energy, pureness.

As you can see, the chakras mix, match and blend into and with the mind, body and spirit. When chakras are in balance we feel and are well. If you get into the habit of balancing, as many people do daily, it ensures the energy ebbs and flows correctly and healthily.

You might already be aware of feelings or sensations in your chakras. If you think of pleasure and passion your sacral area will be perky or maybe described as the ache of lust. However, if you are experiencing grief or sadness you will feel that in your heart. Equally, if you think of love that feeling too will manifest in the same place.

If you experience a shock you may feel knocked for six and this will be in your solar plexus. Please program into your mind that if at anytime you feel threatened or drained by someone's energy gently place your hand or cross your hands over your solar plexus. This will stop psychic attacks or energy leeching. Are you likely to not speak out if you are cross or dissatisfied? Word swallowing will affect your throat chakra.

Your personality is reflected in your chakras as well as your emotional, mental, physical and spiritual self. Your chakra system is the ultimate diagnostic tool and lie detector.

One of my clients had the biggest giggles in the world because she said her sacral chakra was rattling like a bathroom vent. She felt unwanted but it turned out that she always pushed men away thinking they would abandon her. The rattling was a fantastic indication to her to give love a go. I'm very happy to share that she is now happily married.

At one of my salons, the girls were identifying and healing any potential problems in their chakras. Dilys was working on Mands and found a blockage in her sacral chakra. Mands gave her permission to receive healing and to allow unblocking. This was so successful Mands very soon found she was pregnant. This was a fabulous surprise as it was something she and her husband thought might not happen.

At another, Jim shared that he suffered from jealous rages towards his wife, who in reality had never done anything to cause him doubt in her devotion. His blockage showed in his heart chakra and as he was receiving healing he had memory flashes of being let down by a girlfriend who left him for another. He then started to really laugh as this had happened at primary school when he was six. In that instance of realizing it was old unwanted programming, he let it go and became a completely different man! I could go on with successes and stories of change but I expect you would like to get on and take the time to check yours.

A quick interjection here about healing. We are all healers and are all more than capable of directing healing energy to others (when it's wanted). It is purely about intent and nothing more. If a child falls and the mother rubs the injury – that is healing. If someone is crying and you put your arm around him or her in comfort – that too is healing. Not everyone has good intentions and it is important to trust your instincts as to whom you feel comfortable with. You wouldn't let someone cut your hair if you didn't trust and feel comfortable with them, so don't let just anyone into your psyche.

You now have a choice of inner work, using your pendulum or going by what you see or sense. Checking inwardly is best done as a gentle meditation. Sometimes, when beginning this process, emotions are released as tears or laughter. Physical blockages can burst out as coughs or farts. Please blast away to your content: better out than in and all that.

Chakra meditations help you to check the condition of each chakra while healing or releasing any potential blockages or problems. I have created the Chakra Spa for your delectation that once you have visited you will be able to return to at any time you desire.

Your spa is within your mind, but you are able to be within it. It consists of eight very beautiful rooms each with a different theme and healing ability.

You may do this alone, with a friend or in a group. As before, you can read it and let your thoughts drift into it or record it. The complete version is at the end of this chapter.

Chakra Spa

Take a few calming breaths and allow waves of relaxation to wash over you as you sink down into comfort.

In your mind's eye, imagine you are entering the most perfect building. This is your spa and it is exactly how you want it, with every last detail being exactly so. You feel the spa welcoming and beckoning you to go in. When you are in each you room you will be gifted with whatever is necessary for you at that moment.

As you now go through the main entrance enjoy the immediate feeling of comfort and safety and look for the door into the first room – the red one.

As you go through the door, notice any sensations in your body as you are bathed in the red light. Sit in the red chair and take a couple of calm breaths. This room is all about your own security. There are representations personal to you regarding this. When you are balanced here, you are secure, motivated and full of oomph. If all isn't quite well you may be lacking in enthusiasm or feel moody and grumpy.

What are you feeling, noticing or experiencing? Put your attention into your base chakra. Is it clear and free flowing? If it seems mucky or blocked wait a little while for any thoughts to come to your mind as to what is happening. If you need healing in this chakra, the room itself will begin this process. Continue to rest until you know all is well. When you are ready, slowly leave the room and look for the next one – the orange one.

Continue in the same way through all the rooms until you have finished in the violet one. When you are ready, slowly leave the room and look for the next one, the room of unadulterated bliss.

This room has all the colors, but furnished in a gentle way that creates complete calm and absolute bliss. Relax in the chair and slowly draw your attention through each chakra in turn. Detect all the subtle energies and feel immense power in yourself. This power manifests as strength and a sense of well-being.

You may visit your spa at any time and visit each room or just relax in the one you feel drawn to.

When you are ready, bring yourself back. Any processes that have been started off in the spa will continue working away in the background. You might not notice anything going on, but you might get flashes of ideas, memories or vivid clearing-out dreams.

Pendulum on Chakras

Oftentimes, it is useful to have a visual aid representing the condition of chakras and whether there is/are problems in the surrounding areas. This process can be done alone or with another person.

If you are by yourself, sit comfortably and take a few calming breaths. Hold your pendulum over your lap or you can hold it over a photo of yourself. Still and focus your mind as you think about each chakra in order from the base up to the crown. If using a picture, hold the pendulum over the corresponding area on it.

Notice which way your pendulum moves. We want a positive response to show a healthy, clear, free-flowing chakra. If you get a negative movement, put your attention into that chakra and notice what comes to your mind.

Be aware of thoughts, feelings, images, symbols or memories. You will know whether these messages are things you need to work on or if the acknowledgement alone will allow release. As you move up your body you may be aware of shifts or releases and the pendulum may do an array of things to show you the energy changes. Sometimes we just need to let stuff go. Please just go with the flow and allow what will be to happen.

When you have checked all your chakras, note any that aren't showing a positive response and decide what it is you need to do.

When you do this exercise with someone else, you can either have one of you lying with the other holding the pendulum over each chakra, sitting while the other holds the pendulum level with each one, or sitting near each other while you both 'tune in' to each chakra.

They are no definitive rules here, so please do it in the way that you feel comfortable.

If there is a block or imbalance, sending healing will help but, again, the one that is receiving will know if more work needs doing. At the end of the treatment, whether alone or with another, take a few moments to gather thoughts and ensure you are grounded before carrying on with your day.

If you had a block that didn't clear, here is a quick technique to get shift occurring. Ask yourself the following:

What is the problem, issue or difficulty?
How do I know I have this?
What is causing it?
What will happen when this is dealt with?
How will I know it is sorted?
What do I need to do for this to happen?
What shall I do to begin this process immediately?

Here is an example of this in action with someone who had little blocks in her solar plexus and throat chakras:

What is the problem, issue or difficulty?
- I am irritable and snap at the tiniest things.
How do I know I have this?
- I feel my anger welling up and sometimes I am tearful.
What is causing it?
- Tiredness and feeling I have too much to do with not
  enough time.
What will happen when this is dealt with?
- I will be calmer and probably nicer to be around (laughing
  as she replied).
How will I know it is sorted?
- When I feel more in control and stop chasing my tail.
What do I need to do for this to happen?
- Ensure I get enough good quality sleep, be prepared to ask
  for and accept help. I must stop thinking I have to achieve
  everything alone. After all, no one actually cares or
  notices.
What shall I do to begin this process immediately?
- Get some early nights, delegate and book a massage.
The most important part of this method is the actual
  following through and making a start on the plan.

Good intentions are nothing without action. If you like using crystals or stones, the following relate to and can help in the balancing of your chakras:

Base – smoky quartz, garnet, hematite, blood stone.
Sacral – citrine, jasper, gold tiger's eye.
Solar plexus – citrine, amber, topaz, tiger's eye.
Heart – rose quartz, jade, emerald.
Throat – lapis lazuli, turquoise, aquamarine.
Third eye – lapis lazuli, amethyst, sapphire.
Crown – clear quartz, diamond, amethyst.

You can relax with the crystals on their corresponding chakras or, if you are feeling off balance in one area, try having the crystal with you in a pocket or bag.

Chakra Spa Meditation

Settle down now into a comfortable position ensuring that you are warm enough. Take a few calming breaths and allow waves of relaxation to wash over you as you sink down into comfort.

In your mind's eye, imagine you are entering the most perfect building. This is your spa and it is exactly how you want, with every last detail being exactly so. You feel the spa welcoming and beckoning you to go in. When you are in each you room you will be gifted with whatever is necessary for you at that moment.

As you now go through the main entrance, enjoy the immediate feeling of comfort and safety and look for the door into the first room – the red one.

As you go through the door, notice any sensations in your body as you are bathed in the red light. Sit in the red chair and take a couple of calm breaths. This room is all about your own security. There are representations personal to you regarding this. When you are balanced here you are secure, motivated and full of oomph. If all isn't quite well, you may be lacking in enthusiasm or feel moody and grumpy.

What are you feeling, noticing or experiencing? Put your attention into your base chakra. Is it clear and free flowing? If it seems mucky or blocked, wait a little while for any thoughts to come to your mind as to what is happening. If you need healing in this chakra, the room itself will begin this process. Continue to rest until you know all is well. When you are ready, slowly leave the room and look for the next one – the orange one.

As you go through the door, notice any sensations in your body as you are bathed in the orange light. Sit in the orange chair and take a couple of calm breaths. This room is all about your sense of self and your relationships with others. There are representations personal to you regarding this. When you are balanced here you are able to express yourself creatively and are in touch with the feminine and masculine aspects of yourself. If all isn't quite well, you might have a lack of confidence and feel unfulfilled in your relationships.

What are you feeling, noticing or experiencing? Put your attention into your sacral chakra. Is it clear and free flowing? If it seems mucky or blocked, wait a little while for any thoughts to come to your mind as to what is happening. If you need healing in this chakra, the room itself will begin this process. Continue to rest until you know all is well. When you are ready, slowly leave the room and look for the next one – the yellow one.

As you go through the door, notice any sensations in your body as you are bathed in the yellow light. Sit in the yellow chair and take a couple of calm breaths. This room is all about your moods. There are representations personal to you regarding this. When you are balanced here you are able to maintain your energy and disposition whatever life throws at you. If all isn't quite well, you might experience mood swings and feel unstable.

What are you feeling, noticing or experiencing? Put your

attention into your solar plexus chakra. Is it clear and free flowing? If it seems mucky or blocked, wait a little while for any thoughts to come to your mind as to what is happening. If you need healing in this chakra, the room itself will begin this process. Continue to rest until you know all is well. When you are ready, slowly leave the room and look for the next one – the green one.

As you go through the door, notice any sensations in your body as you are bathed in the green light. Sit in the green chair and take a couple of calm breaths. This room is all about love. There are representations personal to you regarding this. When all is well here you are able to express and receive kindness. If all isn't quite well, you may shut yourself off from the affections of others or become overly dependent and needy.

What are you feeling, noticing or experiencing? Put your attention into your heart chakra. Is it clear and free flowing? If it seems mucky or blocked, wait a little while for any thoughts to come to your mind as to what is happening. If you need healing in this chakra, the room itself will begin this process. Continue to rest until you know all is well. When you are ready, slowly leave the room and look for the next one – the blue one.

As you go through the door, notice any sensations in your body as you are bathed in the blue light. Sit in the blue chair and take a couple of calm breaths. This room is all about communication. There are representations personal to you regarding this. When all is well here you are able to express your desires to others and to yourself. If all isn't quite well, you might have trouble with self-expression and withdraw into yourself while depending on others to speak out for you.

What are you feeling, noticing or experiencing? Put your attention into your throat chakra. Is it clear and free flowing? If it seems mucky or blocked, wait a little while for any thoughts to come to your mind as to what is happening. If you need healing in this chakra, the room itself will begin this process. Continue to rest until you know all is well. When you are ready, slowly leave the room and look for the next one – the indigo one.

As you go through the door, notice any sensations in your body as you are bathed in the indigo light. Sit in the indigo chair and take a couple of calm breaths. This room is all about the centre of your intuition. When all is well you are able to use your psychic skills and natural abilities. If all isn't quite well, you might be confused in your mind and put huge focus on materialism while ignoring your instinctive self.

What are you feeling, noticing or experiencing? Put your attention into your brow chakra. Is it clear and free flowing? If it seems mucky or blocked, wait a little while for any thoughts to come to your mind as to what is happening. If you need healing in this chakra, the room itself will begin this process. Continue to rest until you know all is well. When you are ready, slowly leave the room and look for the next one – the violet one.

As you go through the door, notice any sensations in your body as you are bathed in the violet light. Sit in the violet chair and take a couple of calm breaths. This room is all about your spirituality. When all is good you are calm and open to spirit (in your own way). If all isn't quite well, you may feel a sense of separation and lack of purpose or hyperactive as if to justify your existence.

What are you feeling, noticing or experiencing? Put your attention into your crown chakra. Is it clear and free flowing? If it seems mucky or blocked, wait a little while for any thoughts to come to your mind as to what is happening. If you need healing in this chakra, the room itself will begin this process. Continue to rest until you know all is well. When you are ready, slowly leave the room and look for the next one – the room of unadulterated bliss.

This room has all the colors but is furnished in a gentle way that creates complete calm and absolute bliss. Relax in the chair and slowly draw your attention through each chakra in turn.

Detect all the subtle energies and feel immense power in yourself. This power manifests as strength and a sense of well-being.

You may visit your spa at any time and visit each room or just relax in the one you feel drawn to.

When you are ready, bring yourself back. Any processes that have been started off in the spa will continue working away in the background. You might not notice anything going on, but you might get flashes of ideas, memories or vivid clearing-out dreams.

Ground yourself fully before moving onto anything else.

8

Spirit Guides And Angels

Every time we say, 'Let there be!' in any form, something happens.
Stella Terrill Mann

You may already know of your spirit guide or maybe you are sometimes aware of feeling safe and comforted.

Spirit guides are not there to judge you, do things for you or make you do things. They are exactly what it says on the tin – guides. Many mediums and psychics work with their guides and chat with them constantly. This chatting might all be done telepathically or out loud. They could also communicate with a client's guide if the client themselves hasn't or doesn't wish to make contact.

One of my ladies told me she didn't want a guide, as all she could think about was a Native American Indian in a headdress sitting on the edge of the bath while she was on the loo. She had a hard time believing that they aren't interested in watching us brush our teeth or scratch our bums.

Most of us have, at times, called for help in one way or another in the form of a quick silent prayer or incantation: Saint Anthony is often appealed to, to help find lost belongings and Saint Christopher is asked to keep travelers safe. I have heard people say they prayed for help or guidance even if they don't have any kind of belief in God. Then there are the angels: the thought of which, for some, invokes the fear of God, while others get the sensation of love and protection that comes with being taken care of. There are countless stories of 'help' appearing at times of trauma and then the 'help' disappearing immediately after and those might describe the experience as being touched by an angel or somehow, against all the odds, being kept alive until medical help arrived.

The general belief nutshell, with or without a fairy sitting in it, which is a whole other matter, is that a guide has lived as a human and is now in spirit form, while angels have never been alive as an actual human but are within the light.

Angels are beings of a high vibration, but we may use the term angel to describe someone kind, thoughtful or helpful. 'She/he is an angel,' describes a helper and do-gooder; financial angels invest money to help others, and some people seem so angelic that they may be of use if one has slipped off the straight and narrow.

Angels are the connection to our source, and guides help us on the way.

I think the best way to get your head around the subject of angels and guides is to assume they are already with you, but you maybe haven't met them yet, and if you don't want to you don't have to. They will still be there to help you if you ask.

Angels don't really flap about with giant goose wings swooping in to land at your feet if required, even though that is the general depiction of them. The wings are a representation of speed and the shining colors emanate from their auras. Many believe that their vibrational frequency is so high that we don't see them as solid matter, so over time they have been associated with 'coming down from heaven'. How would they get down here if they didn't fly? How indeed! We've all seen religious paintings by the great masters, depicting angels floating about on high and in the past, before the health and safety police stopped all fun, many a child was hoisted onto a platform in the school nativity as they 'flew' down from heaven.

If you see an angel it will probably be as a magnificent huge light form and possibly of many colors. If you feel their presence it will be a feeling of being loved unconditionally and being held safe. They will show themselves to you in a way that you can comprehend and, maybe, if you think the goose wings would help that is what you'll see.

Halos are the colors that show in their auras, so you may see a glowing shape with no specific form. It is unlikely they'll be playing a harp while sitting on a cloud at a cheese spread and cracker picnic.

At times of huge anxiety, a car crash or accident of some kind, an angel can appear as a person to offer help and support. There are many tales of this happening, and Margaret shared the following:

I was driving home late one night in the middle of a noisy storm. I was very tired and desperate to be in a warm bed. The lightening seemed to be continuous and the sky was ablaze with white forks of light cracking down. Despite my need to rush home, I suddenly had the urge to stop. I didn't know why and it was almost as if I was being controlled to do so. As I stopped the car, despite the storm raging all around me, I felt an immense wave of calm and safeness, and the storm sounds seemed muffled. Within seconds, I heard the loudest noise imaginable and saw a tree get struck by lightening just ahead of me in an almost slow motion way. As I watched it crash to the ground my heart was in my throat, as with absolute horror I realized that if I hadn't stopped I would have been under it. And then simultaneously a lorry pulled up behind me and the driver braved the lashing rain to check on me. While I gabbled at him he smiled and then said he'd check the road. He did so and then said he would drive his lorry slowly to the fallen tree and push it out of the way. As he did this, the storm seemed to abate and I watched the lights at the back of his truck move slowly forward and then fade into the distance. I finished my journey and was relieved to get home.

The next day, I drove past the same spot and couldn't

believe my eyes. The tree that had fallen was huge, but it was perfectly laid at the side of the road. There didn't seem to be any evidence of it being pushed by anything, let alone a lorry that had appeared and then disappeared from and to nowhere. As I recall this, it seems dream-like, but I know something unusual happened and feel sure an angel helped me and kept me alive that night.

Angela also shared her story with me:

When I was around eight months pregnant with my daughter, I went to collect my son from nursery. It was pouring down with rain, and I had a coat on with my hood up. I had to walk through a cul-de-sac, which I did everyday and, as you can imagine, it was a very quiet road. I was just about to cross over the road, without looking, when I heard a voice in my ear say, 'Don't cross yet'. I turned my head to look and a car came speeding round the road. I literally had one foot on the road when I heard that voice. After recovering my breath, I looked around but there was no one there. So it was either my sixth sense kicking in to protect me and my baby, or someone from the other side watching over us.

I know it's not an amazing story, but I think about it a lot, and whoever or whatever said that in my ear that day, saved mine and my baby's life, and I will never forget it.

What then of our Higher Selves? This is the part of our being that is within us working in our conscious selves, but able to connect with other dimensions if we so choose. Your higher self has the knowledge of your existence in this and other lives. They are the librarian to your life.

Does all this mean you have to choose the Help Monitor of the day depending where you are or on what you are doing? No, it means help or guidance is available to you any time, any place;

when you trust and ask, you will be able to receive help, healing or guidance. Does it matter who or where from?

If you want to find the name of your spirit guide you can use your trusty pendulum or take a guided journey. What is really cool is to meet your guide and together meet an angel.

If you are dowsing your guide's name, the easiest way is to hold your pendulum over the alphabet. To do this, draw a big circle and make it a pie of thirty-eight sections. Write each letter of the alphabet, numbers one to nine and a zero, and in the remaining two put 'yes' in one and 'no' in another.

Get yourself into the calm focused state and, out loud or in your thoughts, ask if your spirit guide will make him/herself known to you.

Then wait for the pendulum to move to 'yes', or it might start spelling a name. With every response please remember to say thanks in acknowledgement. If nothing happens to begin with, don't worry; just try to relax a little more. Sometimes trying too hard or expecting too much can hinder us. Also, our preconceived ideas can get in the way. Feeling silly or thinking you are talking only to yourself will stop the process being successful.

While you are doing this, you may sense a presence and you may find that you know the answers before the pendulum moves. This is good but again if that doesn't happen it isn't a bad thing. It is all about you getting used to a different way of thinking and receiving answers to your queries.

Some people prefer to meditate and take a guided journey or visualization to meet angels or guides. This can be a gentle enjoyable way to do so.

Here is the outline of a 'meet your guide' meditation. All the meditations follow the same stages: inducing the relaxation, followed by the actual session or reason for the experience. None of it is set in stone, but you will find the more you practise the easier it becomes; your relaxation will happen quicker and soon your awareness will be heightened.

Being calm is necessary for you to make contact with your guides or angels. It is hard for them to break through the fuzzy noise clutter or busy mind if you are stuck in a stressed or anxious state. Likewise, if your thoughts are buzzing with, 'I can't do this', or 'This isn't/won't work', that too will hinder and may intrude on your experience. Entering a meditative state is the answer, as it slows down your stress while also doing a lot of good for your health and well-being. When you meditate, your brain is predominately in the receptive alpha brain wave pattern and it is this that ensures you are at your creative best and open to subtle energy changes around you.

Meditation Journey to Spirit Guide

(The complete script for this is at the end of this chapter.)

Relax into calm comfort and allow everything to slow down.

Imagine waves of calm washing over, in and through you with every moment that passes. With every gentle breath that you take, relax a little more... a little more...

Imagine going for a walk in the countryside, feeling safe and perfectly at ease in your surroundings, as you stroll along the path alongside a field. Take your time appreciating all you see and hear until you find yourself near a log seat. Sit down on it and slowly become aware that you are not alone. You are very comfortable with this and feel a wave of excitement, as you know there is someone sitting next to you. He or she is sitting quietly and waiting patiently for you to become at ease with them being there.

When you are ready, say, 'hello'. If you already know their name, greet them with it. If you don't know what to call them, just ask.

You will know if this person is familiar and you will have time in the future to ask questions, so for now just enjoy the experience. Trust your instincts as to when it is time for you to leave, and as you say 'goodbye', know that now you have met your guide you can communicate with them at any time.

When you are ready, retrace your steps and bring yourself back fully to the here and now.

Take a few moments to awaken fully and assimilate your experience. When you are ready, take a break and do something grounding like having a tea break.

After your break you can take a journey with your Guide to meet your Guardian Angel. Take your time on your break and return for your next journey when you are completely ready. If you prefer, you can wait until another time by reading another part of this book or doing something completely different.

We all have a guardian angel looking after us, as well as other angels that we can call on should we need to. Your Guardian Angel is always with you and will be ready to help if you ask. May I suggest, though, that you don't bark out an angel request if you can't find a product in the supermarket. The other shoppers might fear for their safety and your sanity. However, you may gently be given guidance to where things are by gently enquiring to yourself or being given help on journeys or routes that you are unsure of. You may have thought you were helplessly lost, but then found your way to your destination without really knowing how you managed.

The relationship you pursue with your guides is a very personal one and not really something that can be taught. You will instinctively know what is best and how to proceed. It might be enough to just know they are there or you may wish to communicate regularly with your pendulum or your thoughts.

Making contact with angels is again a private matter. It is possible that you get a full-on light and sound show or a very quite peaceful cozy feeling bathing you in peace and tranquility.

Any of the following might happen to let you know you aren't alone:

The feeling of love.

A smell like a scent of flowers or burning leaves like sage.
A gentle almost undetectable breeze on your skin.
Butterflies in your tummy.
Waves of euphoria.
White feathers left in unexpected places.
...Add your own

On my daughter's wedding day it was pouring with rain. I sat in the car outside the shop where I was about to collect her dress and I asked the fairies and the angels (covering all bases) for it to please not rain while I got the dress, as she got out of the car at the registry office and afterwards while the photos were being taken. At all those times it stopped and in-between it poured. Coincidence? Maybe, maybe not. I still said thank you.

Meditation Journey to Meet Your Spirit Guide

You are about to take a very special journey. Please make yourself comfortable and ensure you are warm enough. You will be fully alert at any time in the event of an emergency, but for now just begin to relax. Take a few regular breaths and imagine beginning to sink down in yourself. Allow your limbs to grow heavy with relaxation like they do when you are sleeping. Slowly move your attention around your body, as each part of you rests and relaxes.

Be aware of how it feels as your feet relax...
Be aware of how it feels as your hands relax...
Be aware of how it feels as your legs relax...
Be aware of how it feels as your arms relax...
Be aware of how it feels as your back relaxes...
Be aware of how it feels as your shoulders relax...
Be aware of how it feels as your neck relaxes...
Be aware of how it feels as your jaw relaxes...
Be aware of how it feels as your face relaxes...
Be aware of how it feels as your head relaxes...

Be aware... of... nothing... in... particular...

Imagine waves of calm washing over, in and through you with every moment that passes. With every gentle breath that you take, relax a little more... a little more...

Sink a little deeper with each and every breath as you feel yourself drifting into peace. Let the reality of day-to-day living float away as you sink into yourself to that special place way down deep inside where all is well. Continue resting while rhythmically counting to yourself as you breathe in and out.

You don't need to alter your breathing pace; just count as you breathe in and allow the number to stay in your mind until you have breathed out fully. Know that by the time you reach ten you will be in a comfortable relaxed state ready to proceed on your journey.

Breathing in on one... breathing out...

Breathing in on two... breathing out...

Breathing in on three... breathing out...

Breathing in on four... breathing out...

Breathing in on five... breathing out...

Breathing in on six... breathing out...

Breathing in on seven... breathing out...

Breathing in on eight... breathing out...

Breathing in on nine... breathing out...

Breathing in on ten... breathing out...

Feel calm. Feel peaceful. Feel relaxed.

Be calm. Be peaceful. Be relaxed.

Imagine now in your mind's eye that you are going for a walk in the countryside. You are safe and perfectly at ease in your surroundings as you stroll along the path alongside a field.

It is a clear perfectly warm day and all is well. You feel at peace with the world as you continue on your walk.

Notice any sounds you might hear. Be aware of everything around you. Take your time as you proceed, enjoy the feeling of freedom and peace. A little way ahead of you are some woods and just before you enter them you will find a log seat that is the most welcoming place to stop and sit, while you gather your thoughts and look around at the beauty of all you can see.

As you rest on the seat, slowly become aware that you are not alone. You are very comfortable with this and feel a wave of excitement, as you know there is someone sitting next to you. He or she is sitting quietly and waiting patiently for you to become at ease with them being there.

When you are ready, turn towards them and say, 'hello'. If you already know their name, greet them with it. If you don't know what to call them, just ask.

Notice if this person seems familiar. Are you surprised? Spend as much time here as you like, either sitting together in quiet contemplation or chatting a little and asking questions. You don't need to rush to discover everything all at once. You will have time in the future to ask more if you choose.

Trust your instincts as to when it is time for you to leave, and as you say goodbye know that now you have met your guide you can communicate with them at any time.

Gently get up and walk away from the seat, back along the path, retracing your steps to the beginning of our walk. When you reach the start, find yourself slowly returning back to the reality of the here and now.

Take a few moments to awaken fully and assimilate your experience. When you are ready, take a break and do something grounding like having a tea break.

Welcome back to the next Journey. This time your guide will be with you while you meet your Guardian Angel.

Hello Angel

Repeat the 'Meet your Guide' meditation, or if you prefer use one of your own relaxations, until you are sitting comfortably on the seat with your guide.

Spend a little while there, just being. There is no need to do or think of anything. This time is yours for you to enjoy new experiences. Think about meeting your Guardian Angel and ask if that may happen.

When you are completely ready, you may notice a bright light or glowing colors appearing in your view. Sometimes, angels appear in vibrant shafts of lights and color. At the same time, there is a feeling of immense peace and love and you may even hear a gentle voice calling your name. The experience will be the one that is right for you. Please accept it without judgment or preconceived ideas.

You will find that you can communicate verbally or telepathically, but you might not want to. You may just want to rest in the magnificence and peace. The role of guides and angels is to be there to care for you and help you through life.

When it is time to leave, say 'goodbye' and 'thanks' then retrace your steps as before. Slowly bring yourself back to wakefulness and gather your thoughts. Make sure you are fully grounded.

9

The Clairs

The beginning of knowledge is the discovery of something we do not understand.
Frank Herbert

Much of what we have already covered is about your inner workings, and your experiences have been guided by your subconscious mind. Although everything you do while developing your psychic and intuitive abilities is easier when you are in a calm relaxed state, for some of the techniques meditation is not always necessary.

It would be useful now for you to discover how you receive information psychically and how you operate intuitively. Everyone has heard of the term 'clairvoyant', but there are other forms of 'Clairs'. You may be proficient in one style but most of us are inclined to a combination.

If you are aware of NLP (Neuro linguistic programming), which is used in therapy for change, release and motivation, you will immediately spot the similarity in identifying sub-modalities as representational systems.

Many NLPers would freak out at the thought of there being these similarities, but if you understand that psyche means the mind, soul and spirit, the worrying can stop and we can all play together nicely.

The Clairs are as follows:

Clairvoyance = clear seeing
Clairaudience = clear hearing
Clairsentience = clear feeling

Claircognisence = clear knowing
Clairangence = clear touching
Clairgustance = clear tasting
Clairalience = clear smelling

When you were tuning in to auras and chakras, you would most likely have seen, felt or just known the structure of the aura and the state and color of the chakras. As you continue to develop your psychic abilities, other senses will join in; so if you get to the stage whereby you are giving someone a reading or healing session, you may get information about that person in different forms. For example, it might be that you saw auras but you sensed how the person was feeling without seeing anything in the chakras.

Clairvoyance

If you are clairvoyant, you 'see' with your third eye chakra as well as your eyes. You see images or symbols in your mind, or you 'see' things that others might not. Images or mind pictures might appear at any time seemingly unrelated to what you are doing or who you are with. By careful observation or by paying attention you will begin to understand and know if you are receiving messages. When the third eye is open, much information is visible when in a meditative state. Some clairvoyants see spirits; if you had a reading to be in touch with a relative who has passed over, you would more than likely visit a clairvoyant. Historical references describe this ability (coupled with telling the future) as having the second sight.

Clairaudience

If you have conversations in your mind or you hear voices of spirits, you are a clairaudient. Some clairaudients hears sounds and voices as if there were someone there and they might or might not see the person or spirit. If you visit someone with this ability, they may well have an actual conversation with sound as opposed to only in thought form. Sometimes, when people begin working with angel energies, they are treated to beautiful melodic sounds.

Clairaudients may also 'hear' your thoughts and feelings; if you spend a lot of time talking to yourself or having imaginary conversations, you will probably use this modality.

Clairsentience

Are you aware of other people's feelings and emotions? It might be that you notice changes in temperature or your tummy lurching in reaction. If so, you are clairsentient. If you tune into others on a sentient level, you might suddenly burst into tears if you pick up immense sadness from them. Likewise, you might detect someone with bad or negative intentions and that can cause a wave of anxiety. If you are detecting spirits or other energies, you might feel 'the touch' like a fine breeze or change in temperature. Empaths are often clairsentient but very finely tuned. Being an empath can be tiring, as they might feel what everyone around them is experiencing and it is beneficial to learn and use ways to switch off or dilute the feelings. This might be easier said than done, but worth practicing if you feel this is what is happening to you.

Claircognisence

This represents 'just knowing'. Have you ever experienced that moment when you know something, yet you have no knowledge of how you know and you can't explain it? It might be that you know when someone has arrived somewhere or you might know that a relative or close friend has been involved in an accident or died. Do you head for the phone or pick up your mobile before it rings? Do you know that a letter is on its way before the postman arrives? If you are tuning into spirits or angels, you know of their presence without necessarily seeing them.

Clairangence

This sense is detecting and receiving information through touch. It is usually referred to as psychometry. This is when people can hold an object and are able to share knowledge on the owner or historical facts like what has happened near the object.

If you are given or buy yourself something second-hand, depending on the previous owner, it might feel positive or negative. You are also able to gather information from standing stones. Funnily though, when you get information from an object, it is often in the form of imagery or fleeting thoughts because all senses work in harmony.

Clairgustance

Can you taste coffee without drinking any or even being anywhere near it? Maybe you are able to taste substances that another person likes if you tune into them. For example, I once heard from a set of twins that each would know what the other was having for supper because they could taste it. This wasn't always pleasing as one loved curry much more than other, but she would get her own back by eating sticky blue cheese, which the curry lover abhorred. If you tune into spirits you may get a sweet taste in your mouth like the little violet sweets.

Clairalience

If you are using this sense, you smell things often that no one else can. Sometimes you might get the briefest whiff of flowers or cigars. If I think about my mother, I can smell freesias, which were her favorites; at other times, I can smell them when there are none about: in the middle of winter, for example.

In the spirit world, smells can be created to alert you to their presence. If you are working with spirits, they can let you know if they perhaps liked a drink or a smoke.

Now you have read through the information on the various

Clairs, you will know how and where you fit. Or, do you? Perhaps you chop and change in various situations. Maybe one is stronger than another if you are tired or very happy. How do you remember people when you first meet them? If you think about someone you love what are you thinking? Are you imagining how they look, sound or their smell?

Do particular sights, sounds or smells trigger memories in you?

The classic is the smell of school dinners. If I smell them now I am transported to a clattering noisy hall with ghastly dinner ladies sending us back to eat the grey unknown slimy substance – vegetables, I believe – swimming in brown matter that purported to be gravy. It did, however, teach me to always be nervous of brown foods unless it is chocolate. At the same time, though, I can recall the smell and taste of delicious sponge puddings with bright, almost luminous, yellow creamy custard – sounds like we were eating nuclear waste doesn't it?

Ideally, it would be great if we could all use all the senses and I think, to a lesser or greater degree, we can. It is possible to enhance any of these abilities if you wish or work on really perfecting the more dominant one or ones you are already aware of.

I mix and match. Sometimes I have seen spirits or time-slip images, but equally I might just know, without seeing anything consciously, where to point the camera to photograph orbs or extra shadows for example. Many people are happy sensing spirits but do not want to see anything in case they get frightened.

My grandsons talk and laugh when there isn't anyone we can see, and various people in the house have sensed and occasionally seen 'extras' – nothing scary though. The best was one morning when Vinnie, my eldest grandson, was about two and was in my living room with Charlie, his mummy and my daughter. They were up early and he was looking through the open door towards the hall, smiling. Charlie assumed that one of us was there hiding in preparation to make her jump. When none of us appeared, she asked Vinnie who was there. 'A horse,' he replied. 'Okay,' thought Charlie. Strange? Not really as we live at Barnfield, so historically it would have been where the horses were kept.

If you are doing a psychic reading for someone, it would help you to know how they process information so you can be on the same level. This brings us nicely round in a full circle back to NLP.

If you give information to someone who is very visual and then ask how that sounds, they might look at you blankly. If you rephrase it to 'how does it look', they will understand immediately.

Recognising your preferred Clair can be achieved with free-flow thinking. This is where you relax a little and let your thoughts wander to wherever they want to. You can drift into a daydream and in it you will know what you are seeing, feeling, touching, knowing, tasting and smelling.

Another technique is to only use one sense at a time. Put an apple or other food substance that you like in front of you and look at it until you get an absolute perfect image of it. Then close your eyes and recreate the image in your mind's eye. Try and make it as vivid as possible. Think about and create the color, the texture and the shape with as much clarity as you can. Then imagine cutting it in half and noticing how it looks inside. Work through all your senses in this way, imagining how it tastes, smells, feels and so on.

When you are an expert, repeat the process but with a person, either by looking at someone until you know exactly how they look or using a photo. Of course, do not do the cutting in half unless you happen to be a magician with a magic box! Instead, think about how the person moves and sounds. In your mind, look at the texture of their hair, skin and clothes. If you are having a conversation with them or they are telling you something, what would they be saying? Hear the level of their voice and the inflections. Be aware of emotions you do or don't feel!

I once led a guided meditation journey with a client called Ralph. I asked him to float above his home and describe what was happening. He related to me that he saw his flat mate, John, arrive at the house, park his car and unload a couple of boxes. He then laughed at his imagination because John was away and he thought he'd obviously made up the whole scene. About an hour after his session, he phoned me in disbelief because he'd arrived home to find that John was there after having cut short his holiday. This had happened at the exact time of the visualization. And the boxes? John had stopped off at work and had been given a computer and printer for home-work.

Why not take yourself on a journey in your mind to anywhere you choose and just notice which bits are easier than others.

Enhancing your skills can be lots of fun and if you decide to do readings you will be even more tuned in.

10

The Oracle

A short saying oft contains much wisdom.
Sophocles

Someone is described as an oracle if they speak with authority and knowledge, often – but not always – in a spiritual way. Oracles were and are present worldwide, but perhaps the most famous was Delphi in Greece. Here, a priestess called the Pythia would pass knowledge that was interpreted and deciphered by priests. Archaeology shows the possibility that there were gases in pockets escaping into the site and that the Oracle would have been drugged by the gas into a trance-like euphoric state. She would then ramble or share visions in response to questions asked, and she held great authority.

However, much like our psychic readings, a lot comes down to interpretation that is dependent on the question or the desire of the seeker. The modern-day Oracle is a seer and someone who reads symbols or looks for clues around them to answer questions from a seeker.

You can be your own oracle with a few tools. Generally, divining the future is the stuff of fairgrounds but it can be a lot of fun, surprising and eye-opening or even all three. As a psychic development tool, divining is valuable as it helps you to focus and fine-tune your mind and senses. People who use tools will often say they don't necessarily need them, but it can be useful to have visual clues and answers. Others will say that when they started to use their tools their psychic-ness grew exponentially.

There are many ways of fortune telling, ranging from

reading tealeaves to cloud formations, runes to scrying, and bones to bird formations, with an astonishing array of other tools in between.

Divining

Here is a very small selection of divination methods of which there are many. Warning – not all are suitable for weak tummies:

Alectryomancy – Through birds

Anthropomancy – Using human entrails

Bibliomancy – With books

Cartomancy – Playing cards

Kephalonomancy - Baked ass's head

Myomancy – Rats

Omphalomancy – The navel

Onychomancy – Fingernails

Pessomancy – Beans

Phrenology – Bumps on a skull

Tasseomancy – Tealeaves

Now, I'm not one to judge, but I did warn you.

Earlier, I talked about Mrs. P and explained that she used to read the tealeaves. As she pointed out and described shapes to me I would nod knowingly, squinting my eyes in the hope of actually spotting something. She would say, 'Can you see that dove flying there? It represents freedom and change'. I would reply, 'Oh yes, I can definitely see that'.

I wished so hard to be able to see a horse-drawn carriage or fairies dancing in the woods, but it was not to be and all I saw were tealeaves. Her dove was my little pile of wet leaves. I didn't get it. However, even though I didn't 'see' a dove I would have the idea of a bird or describe the sensation of flying.

Everyone who saw her thought she was marvelous, as she dished out the tea and advice. Sometimes a cake would be thrown in; critomancy is the divination with cakes in case you were wondering. As it, again, is about the interpretation of signs and symbols, it is probably possible to use anything you fancy. If you think about it, a complete model of psychotherapy has been created using inkblots to define personalities – I rest my case. Perhaps Mr. Rorschach got bored with tea.

There are universally recognized symbols that represent particular ideas, so a blob of one size might mean something almost the same as a blob twice the size, but it is the relationship with all the other blobs that count.

If you are seeking a consensus, that could be difficult as your own interpretations can change with the wind. You might see a heart in the clouds on one day and because of your mood it suggests love is in the air, but a few days later the cloud heart might mean pain and sadness at the end of a relationship. You may look at a flame on Monday that suggests to you butterflies causing excitement in your tummy, but on the Tuesday it reminds you of indigestion.

Signs and symbols can have potent meanings to you that are very personal, but as your awakening continues you will have a better understanding of the hidden implications and possible messages that are about wherever you chose to look. I say 'possible' because a dollop of cloud could be just that – no reason, no secrets, just the way the water droplets are hanging in the air while they try to decide whether to pee on your parade.

When I was young, I used to watch shapes forming in the flames of the fire and thought they were dancing only for me. It was very soporific and I would spend so much time fire-gazing that my parents would tell me to move away before I cooked. Shamans and witches look for signs within the flames of fire and add substances to cause flashes and color changes that can also have meaning.

Runes are always good to use for answers, or even questions, and seem to work better if you gather your own pebbles or small pieces of wood and draw shapes on them like I did for the school fete using a waterproof marker pen. There are a few different runic alphabets, but if they are for personal use you could design the symbols for, for example, a house, success, money, love, freedom, career, numbers or letters of the alphabet, plus whatever else you like. When you have made your own, put them in a little bag and then either draw out a fixed amount, usually three, or throw the whole lot up and take a reading from the ones that land face- or picture-up. Trust your instincts on the messages you receive. Runes usually give good clues to what is happening in the present moment and what it might be useful for you to think about or focus your energies on.

You really don't need anything too fancy to get fantastic results. If you really get into the enjoyment of rune reading then it will be time to research an actual runic alphabet that you resonate with and create a new lot.

A crystal ball is pretty much compulsory in the psychic's house and can be as much for decoration as use, because they are aesthetically pleasing and irresistible to gaze into. When my daughter, Charlie, was about ten, she looked into one and saw a chain. As her description continued, it became clear that she was actually describing DNA, which is a rather perfect way to begin. Like any form of scrying or fortune telling, the symbols remain similar, but as the object itself is the focus they are presenting in a different way. As you gaze at or into the item it will induce a focused state of mind and the things you see are in your mind's eye as well as in the actual ball or similar.

When I look into my crystal ball, it can be like watching a film with hazy edges, while at other times I get flashes of images but am not always sure whether they are in the ball or in my mind. I am fortunate that nowadays I can just plonk mine anywhere, but if you prefer ritual: a plain cloth, traditionally dark velvet is placed under the crystal ball. It is important to ensure it is clean before it is put on the cloth and a rinse under running water is the best way. Don't let anyone else touch your crystal ball, but if it's unavoidable make sure you clean it before you read from it. Remember to dry with a lint-free cloth or you'll be lint-reading and who knows what the fluff might tell you?

The most successful results tend to be in dim or candlelight as this allows our mind to be calm and we can then see images that in full daylight might be lost in the brightness. Place your ball on the velvet cloth and sit a comfortable distance from it, making sure you can see into it without straining. Be calm and have your question in your mind as you start to lose focus. Should you see a movie burst forth or hear a trumpet fanfare start up, try not to jump. Let what needs to happen, happen. If nothing is going on, don't worry as there's always next time.

A good thing to try out is to think of someone you know when you look into the ball and see what the ball shows you. A bowl of water works perfectly well if you haven't a ball, as does a mirror. Scrying mirrors are usually black and readers may also sprinkle a few drops of ink or dye into a bowl of water for the same effect. A dark colored bowl will suffice instead. Try out various ways and you'll soon discover your forte.

Here is a reading from a Salon carried out using a bowl of water:

The two girls had never met before the day. The reader did not know anything about the seeker and had no idea of her question. With nervous giggles to begin, they shook hands to form a bond and the reading began.

Reader: 'I'm sensing a pile of rubble and a feeling of frustration. There is a cat sitting on the pile staring intently, but I don't know what it is looking at. That has gone and I can see an operating table with a scalpel on it. Everything is calm. Oh, now there is a ring – a wedding band. Hang on; it's changing into a sort of heart with a crown. I am getting "glad" or "clad" – oh, I'm not sure – and I feel I want to say "glad rags", but don't think that is right. It's a similar sound I'm hearing.'

This girl continued to share, getting more and more information with the other girl silenced into disbelief, until she said 'glad rags', at which point she burst into tears. A silent hush filled the room as everyone stopped to listen.

The girl's question was, 'would her fiancé propose soon?' This is a common one – the pursuit of love.

After taking a few moments to compose herself, the girl explained that her boyfriend was renovating his house for them to live together; they had a running joke, whenever she visited, that the cat loved her more than him. She had recently had a minor operation and it had gone very well with excellent results.

The part that had set her off, though, was the ring. She had just heard a Claddagh ring being described: an Irish wedding band. Yes, he was Irish and, yes, he did propose.

All that from a bowl of water is pretty amazing, I think. The girl doing the reading had really opened up her psyche and gone with the flow. She shared what she saw or sensed without analyzing or putting her own spin on things. This is the best way. Always!

Is it time for you to have a go? Gather your equipment; clear your mind; relax your breathing and let your eyes gently unfocus as you gaze into your preferred tool. What do you see?

Here to get you started are some of the general symbols and meanings, which are also relevant to tea-leaves, coffee grounds, sand and mud:

Anchor, upright = stability. If upside down = inconsistent
Apple = good health
Baby = new starts or pregnancy
Ball (circle) = completion

Boat, big, shiny, fast = success. If broken or sinking = floun-
  dering or confusion
Bell = spirituality, good news
Bridge = finding the way
Butterfly = transition
Candle = new starts
Cat = luck or deceit
Chain = strength, linking together as in a wedding, DNA
Clock = time passing
Cloud = movement, freedom
Coffin = endings, final (not death)
Coin = success coming or going
Dagger = danger
Dog = friendship
Door, open = new starts. If closed = endings or finalizing
Dove = freedom, change
Duck = fun and noise
Egg = new starts
Elephant = security, wisdom
Envelope = message or news – good or bad
Eye, open = creation. If closed = not seeing something
Feather = spirituality
Fence = block or limitations, trapped
Finger = being beckoned or directed
Fire = spirituality
Fork = choices or falseness
Forked path or line = choices
Fruit = abundance, prosperity
Gate, open = success. If closed = trapped, needing another
  way through
Gun = fear, anger
Hammer = hardship
Hand, open = friendship. If closed = arguments
Harp = harmony, love

Hawk = jealousy

Heart = pleasure, love or grief

Horseshoe = good luck, success

Hourglass = time passing by

House = security

Jewels = gifts

Kite = freedom

Ladder = rising (usually career)

Leaf = newness

Line, straight = forward progress. If jagged or wavy = challenges ahead

Lion = strength

Lock, closed = blocked. If open = new beginnings. Lock and keys are associated with sex.

Loop = repetition

Mask = hiding

Mountain = obstacle or challenge

Mushroom = rise upwards or frustration

Nail = unfair

Needle = joining

Oak leaf or tree = strength, longevity

Octopus = danger, choices

Owl = knowledge

Palm tree = success

Parasol, open = insight or protection. If closed = something hidden

Parrot = talking

Pig = greed or success

Purse = profit or loss

Question mark = ask the questions

Rabbit = need to be brave

Raven = news, sometimes bad, but offering new beginnings

Ring, whole = joining or marriage. If broken = ending

Rose = love or being pricked by a thorn

Saw = separate
Scale = legal matters or balance
Scissors = quarrels
Sheep = good luck
Shell = good news
Shoe = new starts or journeys
Snake = knowledge or sly
Spider = togetherness
Star = happiness and health
Sun = success, power
Sword = arguments
Table = gather or talks
Tortoise = slowness, methodical
Tree = strength and new starts
Triangle = surprise or power
Waterfall = prosperity
Wheat sheaf = abundance
Wheel, whole = success. If broken = sadness
Wings = messages
Wolf = jealousy or security

As you can see, even though the whole idea of signs and symbols is right-brain thinking, the meanings associated with objects and shapes are logically left-brained. A tortoise would suggest slowness and a sword would suggest arguments – so, no surprises really.

You will also have noticed that several signs, pictures and symbols have opposite meanings. It doesn't necessarily matter which way up they are either, as it is the general thought and relationship with other signs. Also, a blob, although not looking like the wolf, triggers the thought of one or the feeling of security and protection in the form of unconditional love. You are not looking for a photographically clear picture. With any kind of divination, the usual way is to have a question in your mind rather than just start looking.

I am not really au fait with the reading of rats or entrails, so can't offer any advice if that is your inclination, but bring on the teapot and away we'll go.

Reading the Tealeaves

Brew up a cup of tea without milk and without using a strainer. If you haven't got a teapot, the cheat's way is to split a teabag and pour on hot water. Even though black tea might not be your pleasure, just take a couple of sips. This is important to allow your 'you-ness' to be part of the process. When you have finished, tip the remainder away and quickly tip the cup and turn it three times, clockwise, bringing it to rest upside down on the saucer for a few moments.

Clear your mind and, as you turn the cup the right way, take a couple of calm breaths. Allow images to float into your mind. You might look at the dregs and see shapes immediately. Is the dove there? You may see suspicions of shapes or it might be that the tealeaves trigger thoughts and images in your mind. Go with the flow. If you wish, you can write down everything that you see or think and interpret it afterwards rather than attempt a full-on analysis straight away. This process works with coffee if you prefer and even fruit juice with the bits. As you proceed you will discover many other symbols and you will know their meanings intuitively, whether they seem obvious or not. You might see a sprig of rosemary and it may well elicit thoughts of food, healing a sore throat or sitting in a taverna by the sea on a Greek Island. Guess what it does to me?

Also, the images may set off other senses depending on your inner workings, so the scent of flowers may drift to you as you look at a clod that could resemble a rose. The important thing is to keep it lighthearted and fun.

Sand, salt or earth is good to use too. Sprinkle a small pile onto a tray and play with it. Pass it from hand to hand and let it flow between your fingers. When ready, gently level the tray with a couple of slow side-to-side movements before resting it on a level surface. What do you see?

Why not try ink? Liquid ink or a split cartridge will work beautifully. Just drop or flick it onto blotting paper or even draw or paint on one-half of a piece of paper and fold it into a butterfly image. What is it now? Two vases or a face, a well-endowed man or the head of an old hag?

When you are reading for (or working with) someone else, make sure they keep their question or the information they are seeking to themselves until after you have shared your findings. Don't be put off if it seems way off. I have heard stories whereby something has happened months after and the person remembers what they saw.

As always, it is perfectly acceptable to ask for guidance from your guides.

11

Mind Whispering

Most folks are about as happy as they make up their minds to be.
Abraham Lincoln

Before we move on, I would like to talk about the power of your mind and how you, yourself, can create success in everything you do. When you are awakening your psychic abilities and intuition, it is important to have positive thoughts and surround yourself with positive energies. This should be from your surroundings and the people you spend time with. Psychic vampires drain and tire us. If you spend time with miseries you will become one if you're not careful and aware of yourself. By slightly shifting your thought processes, you can make amazing changes in yourself with just the whispers in your mind.

We mostly have a dialogue going in our mind telling us what we should or shouldn't be doing, how we can or can't manage or even why we must or mustn't be doing something. Negativity in any form feeds on itself and grows more and more powerful as it does so. Positivity also grows with little encouragement, but sometimes it can be elusive if doubts or fears are present.

Please remember that any negativity only has power if you grant it, and when you decide it cannot exist in you it really won't be able to.

Think of a time when you felt and knew that you looked good: one of those days when all was well and you were fortuitous. Perhaps you were smiled at or someone gave you a compliment that immediately made you feel even better and more confident.

Now remember a time when you felt a bit daggy: bad hair

day, squidgy bits day, not getting enough done from the 'to do' list or similar. On that day, it is likely someone may have told you that you looked tired or asked you if you were feeling poorly. They might have been that incredibly witty person that said, 'Cheer up, it might never happen'. Well done if you didn't growl at them, but even that comment was someone's attempt to help you or cheer you up.

What then makes one day so good and another so rubbish? Why and how can you feel so different from one to the next? Why isn't every day perfect and brilliant?

It is because of what happens in your mind. On the good days, your self-esteem is high; your confidence is untouchable and your self-belief is on top form.

On a bad day, your mind whispered to you and it wasn't good. This can happen even when someone comments on your appearance in a positive complimentary way. We can receive praise repeatedly, but still dismiss it disbelievingly because we know differently or better. The positive person gets it from themselves. You can't buy it or take a pill for it. It might take a bit of practice but, like any habit, it is attainable by everyone.

Have you ever tried to change something? Like giving up smoking or getting over a phobia, for example? And what happens? Probably not a lot because, again your mind whispers, 'You can't!' So, you don't.

Those who are successful whisper to themselves that they can do things or change something if it isn't right. You, no doubt, know people who exude confidence and happiness. And, equally, you probably know those who don't. They always seem to fail or spend time saying, 'can't' or 'shouldn't'.

What are Mind Whispers? They can be that little voice or perhaps that not-so-little voice when it really gets carried away with itself. They may be thoughts, images or feelings. But, however they manifest to you, the first thing to realize is that you have created them based on your knowledge and experience of life. And, therefore, only you can change them.

If you are attempting to meditate, see auras or meet a spirit guide, if you whisper that you can't you will get your wish. But, please don't think that just because you haven't managed something in the past it means that you can't now, as with a little work and a tweak of your thoughts you can!

The easiest way to either make change and/or become positive and successful is to be aware of your own mind whispering. When you have done this, you will find that everything becomes more fluid. You will become more aware of your intuition and inner abilities. Also, your senses will be enhanced.

Imagine now stepping aside from yourself and becoming a casual observer or listener to your thoughts. What are you saying to yourself? Try and drop in on yourself a few times each day and notice the pattern that you follow. Do you like what you hear? Are your whispers those of success?

If they are, that is fantastic: cheers to your achievements. If they aren't quite what you were hoping for, you can change them.

Every time a bit of negativity or doubt creeps in, spend a moment acknowledging it and then rephrase in the positive. Hear your mind say, 'I can. I am. I will'. Say to yourself, daily, the moment you wake up, 'I am successful, healthy and happy in mind, body and spirit'. Keep saying this until it gets in a loop that plays constantly in your mind.

One of the first known affirmations was created at the turn of the twentieth century by the pharmacist and psychologist Émile Coué, who taught people to repeat, 'Every day, in every way, I'm getting better and better', morning and night. Try this 'Couéism' and notice what happens after just a few days.

When you practice being positive and encourage yourself to live a life of abundance, your subconscious mind will ensure that it happens. And if life knocks you back: get up, dust yourself down and start again.

It can also be revelatory to notice the whispers of others. You can tell by their behavior and from the things they say. Tiny little comments can have such a profound effect to the good or bad. One of my clients, Liz, made amazing changes in her life, despite having the mother of all negativity. Her mother always managed to create doubt in Liz or lower her confidence and it wasn't until she was in her thirties that it actually dawned on her what was happening. On this particular day, Liz and her husband were visiting on their way to see his parents. She was worried before they even arrived as she knew a mean comment would be made even though Liz had done a pregnancy test that morning and was carrying the happiest news. They arrived at her mother's house to be greeted with, 'That's a nice dress, but was that really the only belt you could find?' Liz felt deflated and burst into tears. Her mother seemed confused by this reaction, but then confessed that she even knew she did it but something always seemed to make her. After a heart-to-heart over a cup of tea, it became clear that the mother had been brought up to 'not be big-headed', to 'not get ideas above her station', plus a few other cliché sayings and felt she had to treat her own daughter in the same way. For how many generations might that have gone on if Liz hadn't snapped that day? They are best friends now and Liz's daughter has the kindest, most positive grandma imaginable.

I am not suggesting that you launch an attack or weep a river onto anyone who is negative. My desire is that you only let the positive flow your way and bounce negativity straight back. While you are demonstrating success in your life, which you will as you develop psychically, others might be jealous or try to lower your self-confidence. If you notice that happening, just smile inside and be full of positive light. This light will spread and may even begin to help those miseries.

Here is a beautiful mediation for you. It is the script for Your Special Place. I teach this to my clients and it is always well-received.

Special Place Script

This script can be used as it is or you can use it as a guide to create your own.

You can memorise it, record it or have someone read it to you.

Pause at the ellipsis (...)

Make yourself comfortable with your arms and legs uncrossed; ensure that you are warm enough and will be undisturbed for the duration of your session.

Begin

Close your eyes and pay attention to your breathing. Try to make the out-breath last a little longer than the in-breath. Only do this in the way that you feel comfortable.

Focus your attention on just you...

Imagine now that your legs are relaxed from the knees down and each time you breathe out... feel a wave of relaxation wash over you and through you with every breath...

All sounds that you hear, apart from an emergency, remind your mind that you are relaxing. If you need to awaken, you may do so immediately and you will feel alert and refreshed.

But, for now just enjoy...

Spend a few moments thinking about how you would know, what you would experience, what you would feel if your legs were more relaxed than they had ever been...

Only you can experience your relaxation...

Imagine now that your arms are relaxed from the elbows down...

And, all the while, your breathing is becoming slower and slower...

Gentle, comfortable regular breathing...

Spend a few moments thinking about how you would know, what you would experience, what you would feel if your arms were more relaxed than they had ever been...

Only you can experience your relaxation...

Now, you can allow the relaxation in your lower arms and lower legs to spread and flow upwards as you now feel your arms and legs relax completely...

You have no need to think of anything or nothing but if you wish you may think of everything or something...

The relaxation in your legs can now begin to flow gently up through your hips, pelvic area, tummy and chest...

The relaxation in your arms can spread out across your shoulders, and slowly, gently but very thoroughly down your back...

All that relaxation can now flow up, into your face, up the back your head, all the way to the very top of your scalp...

And then, gently, like waves on the sand, calming peaceful relaxation can wash all the way back down your whole being...

Everything is slowing down... Every part of you is relaxing...

This is your time... time just for you... to rest... and... relax...

Mentally scan your mind and body for any tensions or anxieties...

If you come across any, mentally massage and soothe them away.

Resting now... Feeling peaceful...

... ...

Imagine now that you are standing at the top of some steps that are leading down towards a door.

We are now going to slowly, carefully walk down the stairs, counting from one to ten as we go.

As we go down each step, with each number, feel yourself relaxing more and more deeply.

Let's begin going down...

One, slowly, gently going down...

Two, allowing yourself to feel calm and peaceful...

Three, everything relaxing more and more...

Four, slowing down...

Five, breathing out tensions, worries, fears and anxieties...

Six, slowly, carefully, going down the steps. Relaxing even more...

Seven, think of a word that you associate with being calm and relaxed...

Eight, and say this word inwardly to yourself every time you breathe out...

Nine, continue to say your word. And every time you hear your word in your mind you relax even more deeply...

Ten, you can carry on resting using your word and continuing to feel calmer and calmer...

Stand in front of a door now that is at the bottom of the stairs. It is closed, but in a moment you can go through the door and find yourself in your special place.

Go through the door now and be in that special place.

This special place is the place that you are creating just for you. It is a place within you that you can be within. In this special place, all is well.

You can visit your special place whenever you choose to. Spend some time now having a look around. Make sure it is all exactly as you want.

The following suggestions can go into your inner mind, repeating without you needing to think of them consciously.

All is well.

You are healthy, fit and strong in mind and body.

You can make any and all changes that you desire, on all levels of your being, because you have control of you.

You can release anything within you that is not serving a purpose.

You are free.

Add any positive thoughts of your own that you wish to put in to your mind for you to make any changes you desire.

Be clear in your mind. Create specific images.

Imagine how you will feel, look, and all the things you will experience when you have accomplished your goal/s.

Have total belief that you can achieve everything you set out to achieve.

Imagine now that you are 'there'. It's good isn't it?

Enjoy the experience.

And, when you are ready and only when you are ready, gently bring yourself to an awake state by counting in your mind, three, two, and one – awaken.

Take a few moments to gather your thoughts and ensure that you are fully grounded.

Your Mind Whispers will win in any situation or circumstance. Use yours wisely.

12

Past Life Regression

It's a poor sort of memory that only works backward.
Lewis Carroll

Beyond Bliss attendees are usually very keen to explore their past-life memories and sometimes they have questions forming for themselves to discover. They may have snippets of information already tapping on their subconscious door from the aura and chakra work. When we do the times and places exercise, they often begin to notice a pattern and things begin to fall into place before we even get to the regression meditation.

How often do we hear of people having déjà vu about places? So many of my clients describe the feeling of familiarity on visiting somewhere for the first time, even to the point of being able to describe what is around the next corner of the layout of a building.

We can easily be holding onto unnecessary emotional debris from our past that has absolutely no purpose or value now. It doesn't even seem to matter what personal belief structure is in place with regards to unearthing memories of other lives. Beliefs vary from soul recall, genetic programming, cell memory, metaphor, vivid imagination, ancestral knowledge, through to the collective unconscious. Wherever you are on the belief ladder is personal and right for you. The thing to note is that regression can be very illuminating. It can give us answers to aspects of ourselves and our behaviors: releasing fears and phobias, worries or anxieties.

I once had a client who stuffed herself with bread whenever she could. She spent most of her time avoiding it, but if she saw any, or worse if she smelt some, she lost control and would gorge until she hurt. In her regression, she recalled being starving and stealing bread from the market. Unfortunately, she was caught and killed. On the surface, it would seem to make more sense if she were to avoid bread now but her mind had suppressed the memory of being caught and killed, so the program she was running on was still one of starvation and survival. When she recalled the truth, she admitted that she didn't actually like bread and it was a huge relief for her to no longer be enticed by it.

I have worked in the area of past-lives for many years, or even lifetimes. Teaching people to access their other lives and exploring memories can be a fabulous experience that can bring pleasure, answers, questions, release, change or the feeling of 'ahha'. In a group, I might not know the memory that has been uncovered or remembered, but the expressions and comments say more than enough. Many times, I see heads nodding knowingly. Others start laughing as suddenly they 'get it'.

Remembering my own memories changed my life quite literally. I have already mentioned the saga of my back and operations, and here are a couple of excerpts from my book, *Past Life Tourism*, which seem to tie my loose ends:

As with all good lessons, in order to get the most from them it is best to experience them firsthand. So, I watched somewhat nervously as a couple of other students and guests were regressed and, without any shadow of doubt, I knew my first regression would reveal that I was Boudica or Cleopatra or another powerful woman of note. Can you therefore imagine my astonishment at discovering I was working as a prostitute in a bar?

I could see in my mind's eye the layout of the bar and knew it was in Louisville. Under the instructor's guidance, RS questioned me excitedly while I talked about the cowboys, who it seemed I did not like at all, sitting around being raucous, spitting chewed tobacco and drinking. I was in the business to support my little sister as we had no parents and although I didn't know what happened to them it wasn't an issue. To my horror, I discovered I was pregnant. Not good when you have to make your money with your body.

RS took me forward to the time of the birth and asked me who was president. Fool, I thought!

My reply was, 'I'm about to give birth to a bastard child and you're asking me that!' As I gave birth, I told him the president was Lincoln.

It was quite upsetting to the 'me' in the now that anyone, let alone myself, would call a baby something so awful. This was a powerful indication to me about how different we can be in other lives.

I recalled that the baby turned out to be a girl, who I loved immediately, and soon after I was living happily with a wonderful man, my daughter and my sister.

At the time I was pretty sure that none of that would have been in my life script, but after I'd recovered it made complete sense. It was like a little bit of my own life's jigsaw had slipped into place. I'm whispering this bit – deep down I've always thought I'd make a rather good Madam!

And later...

After all these dramatics, I then developed an intermittent stage fright. Intermittent I hear you cry? Yes. A 'now and then' type fear. It was more stressful than having a full-on phobia. I didn't think that experience had given me the problem; it just reminded me it was in my psyche somewhere.

I tried various things on myself then, in a flash of inspiration, wondered if it was a past life issue intruding. I recalled a memory of being a dancer. There weren't any specific dates but I could smell sweat and makeup. I had David Bowie's 'Diamond Dogs' playing in my head, and as I'm writing this it has just come on in iTunes. It all seemed overtly sexual and I could sense lots of red velvet, and I knew I was wearing frilly knickers. My name was Rose and the name Charles Sidle (or similar) was in my mind.

In my memory I was given the chance to be a front performer, but stumbled and severely hurt my back. Useless, then, as a dancer. I was back selling my body; same old me again! I know now the name I was sensing was Zidler and it was the Moulin Rouge. The music playing was a clue from this life – presented to me as a metaphor.

Diamond Dogs was the name given to the prostitutes. And, after all, diamonds are a girl's best friend – it's not a dog, Touch éclat or GHDs. Imagine if David Bowie was one of my customers in a past life. Excuse me a minute while I have a quick fantasy.

Who knows whether all of this was my creative imagination or I really did Can-Can and land in the splits with my drawers on show. All I can say is that now I help people get over their stage fright and occasionally have the urge to lift up the front of my skirt.

Just two short examples show how our lives have threads and themes that we weave and replay, and the amazing power of how we create our circumstances to fit our own life plan. Not all past-life recalls are associated with problems or difficulties. For example, Martha discovered she could paint and Albert was multi-lingual while visiting their pasts: both were able to utilise their skills in the here and now. Many have discovered the reasons for obsessions and interests in people, places or objects and, likewise, reasons for their distastes or repulsions.

Times and Places
Spend a while thinking of places in the world that you are attracted to or maybe even feel nervous about. I have an obsession with Greece that I had no awareness of until my first visit. I met the vice-consulate's secretary in the supermarket

while in Kos (like you do) and we started to chat. Before we had paid for the shopping, she had invited me to tea to tell me everything I needed to know should I decide to live there. When you hear tales of people visiting a place and staying put I wonder if they are returning to their roots and almost haven't a choice.

Whenever I fly into Athens, as the plane floats gracefully down over the port of Rafina, it feels like I'm returning to my spiritual home.

After you have thought about places, and you can be as detailed as you like, by narrowing your focus from a particular country to a town or area, move your mind to times in history that you like or don't. Are you attracted to Ancient Egypt or the Tudors, Romans or particular wars? This might tie into thoughts about styles of clothing.

This exercise can be as long and thorough as you choose. You can list places, times, people, foodstuffs, even colors.

What about anything you might be holding in your chakras: emotions or unresolved aches and pains. Think about birthmarks or other marks on your skin. Have you fears or anxieties but don't know why? Are you attracted to trying something new or different but haven't pursued it for fear of failing or ridicule?

Any of these things might be relevant (or equally mean nothing whatsoever) as your mind will recall what is useful or beneficial to you now. It is this that can make memory recall so much fun.

Of course, if you prefer, you don't need to do any preliminary thinking; you can go straight into your regression and see what comes up. This way round is preferable to many, as they prefer the 'surprise'.

If you have read *Past Life Tourism*, you are already an expert on regressing and if you had anything to sort or deal with you have probably done so. If you have, please proceed onwards in this book, but you are welcome to recheck that your inner filing is in order.

The following meditation will help you remember anything that might be useful to you now or in the future. You can read it to yourself, record it or have someone else read it to you. If you are alone, doing an eyes open meditation, just ignore the instruction to close your eyes. As with all relaxations, please pause at the ellipses.

Your Past Life Journey

At all times you are in control and you will get the most benefit if you use your imagination as best as you can. If you are looking at something and you aren't physically seeing anything, just use your senses and imagine what you might see, hear, feel, taste, smell or sense.

Okay. Get cozy and make sure you are warm enough. This meditation is gentle and calming. To begin, you will physically relax and then, as your mind rests, you will be able to focus your thoughts more and more to retrieve your memories. From now on during this process, all noises and sounds that you hear, apart from an emergency, just remind your mind that you're relaxing. If you need to awaken you can do so at any time. But, for now...

Let's begin. Imagine that, as you are breathing, gentle calming waves of relaxation are rhythmically flowing through you.

Beginning at your feet. As you breathe in, imagine the feeling of relaxation flowing into your feet. Really get into the rhythm. As you gently breathe in and out, the relaxation washes through, in and over you like waves on the sand. With each breath, the waves flow higher... your breathing controls your relaxation. As you breathe out fully, you rest even more, even more. Allow the wave to flow now... to your knees... thighs... hips... tummy... chest... up your back... neck... shoulders... everything resting, slowing down and now the calm and spread up into your face and head...

And now... slowly, gently but very thoroughly, back down your body like little waves on the sand.

Calm. Peaceful. Relaxed. Soothed. Taking yourself down inside yourself to where you feel comfortable. That cozy feeling way down deep inside, where all is well. This is your time now – time for you.

Any tensions, anxieties, worries or fears are mentally massaged away. Draining away from you.

Think about floating with relaxation as you sink deeper...

As you relax more and more deeply I am going to count from one to ten and you can allow the passing numbers to help you to rest even more... even more...

One, resting... relaxing...

Two, breathing gently... relaxing more and more with every breath... with every gentle beat of your heart...

Three, be soothed... caressed in peace...

Four, breathe away any tensions or anxieties...

Five, rest... relax... calm...

Six, calm... breathing easy... soothed...

Seven, resting more and more deeply...

Eight, inner peace washing over you and through you... calm... peaceful... relaxed...

Nine, each breath taking you deeper and deeper into calm and peace...

Ten, continuing to relax...

And now... be in your special place. It can be somewhere that you know or somewhere that you make up. It can be inside or out. Use your imagination as best you can. Have your special place exactly as you like... colors... textures... everything perfect...

All that matters is that this special place is yours – it belongs to you. You choose who or what you have there. Relaxing now, in that special place within you, that you are now in. Spend some time looking around... enjoy the feelings and inner contentment...

In your special place there is a door that leads outside. The door is only there when you want it to be there.

Go to the door now, and if it is closed gently push it open and step through it, onto the small safe step that leads onto the bridge of time. You are safe and in control as we slowly cross over the bridge to your past. Sense the swirling pale blue mist that you are walking through and pause when you are half-way.

Now slowly continue over the bridge and notice that the mist is gently clearing on the other side. As you step off the bridge, you have traveled back in time to a memory of significance in one of your past lives. Take a moment and wait for the mist to clear.

Take your time and get your bearings.

Allow yourself to tune in to where you are. Remember you are just looking... in a safe, detached way.

Begin to notice things now – are you inside or outside? Is it quiet or is there noise? Are you male or female? What season is it? You can explore while I continue to prompt your thoughts, but you don't particularly need to listen to me.

Become aware of your thoughts and feelings associated with whatever you experience. Are there other people about? What are you wearing? Can you sense colors, textures, temperature? Do you know your name?

Take your time to really allow your senses to detect everything.

If there are other people about, are they familiar to you?

Now you can travel in time through the memory to events or happenings that are relevant to you. Perhaps you are receiving an answer or an indication of why something is as it is. Do not be concerned if the chronological order of time is muddled – you will be able to sort through later and it will make sense.

If you are seeking something in particular that you would like resolved, go now to the time where that answer awaits. You are safe and detached. If you are not seeking anything in particular, just explore.

Gather the information you desire, but know you don't have to do it all in one go, and it may well be that knowledge comes to you in your daydreams or dreams of the night.

If you find an emotion attached to a memory that isn't useful or productive, detach from it now. In your mind, acknowledge it, thank your mind for enabling you to discover this and then imagine separating from that emotion. Knowledge is very valuable and often just knowing is all that we need.

Take yourself now to near the end of that life. Become aware of all that is happening. Your location, your thoughts, feelings, emotions. Are you alone or with others? What is happening around you?

Now go beyond the moment of passing from that life – be free.

Sense the clearness. Look or think back to that life you've just been recalling and know that there is an important message or learning for you. Wait until you have that valuable insight...

You will bring that back with you. Be peaceful and restored.

It is time for you to return now. Find yourself back on the bridge of time and slowly cross back towards now. Feel safe and calm. As you step off the bridge, leave the past where it belongs – in the past – just a memory like any other memory. Keep hold of the valuable message that you have.

Come back through the door and into your special place.

Find somewhere to rest while you assimilate whatever you have gathered.

Make sure all your inner filing is done and know that you can return whenever you choose or you may retrieve other memories.

It is now time to awaken – bring yourself awake as I count from ten to one.

Ten, nine, eight, seven, six, five, four... more and more

awake...

Three, two, one... eyes open, have a stretch and if you like make notes on your experience.

How was that? When in a group, there is always a fascinating discussion following a regression. If you had a blockage in a chakra before the meditation now might be a good time to recheck and balance.

If you are interested in researching the information you recall, whether for validation or interest, here are some things for you to be aware of during your regression. Some of the answers you will already know, others you may have to look for even though you might not always find the answers the first time. You will, perhaps, have other thoughts and ideas if you are seeking something in particular. You can guide without leading. If you read through the list before you regress you will trigger your mind to make a mental note of the answers. If you are working with someone they can be asked as direct questions.

Marital status – maiden name/own name/known as?*

Are there children and if so are they yours?

Important buildings/monuments/places/people?

Senses: taste, smell, sounds?

When – season/date/year?

How/where traveling to or from?

Fears or pleasures?

Weather?

Food you are having or that you can see?

Age?

*When I asked one client his name I got nothing back, so I asked what those nearby called him. The aggressive reply was, 'Sir!'

Knowledge of a past life can become clearer with time or you might only remember it for a short while in the same way that a dream can be so clear and vivid, yet within minutes you can't remember any of it. Like dreams, certain triggers can bring a memory to the forefront of your mind. Dreams can tie in with our past and our futures and many times, when people have experienced a past life regression, they will get more memories appearing to them during sleep. These can also be predictive of what is to come. If you are interested in dream analysis try having a notepad next to your bed and if you awaken in the night, or when you first wake in the morning, note down any thoughts you have. This will work even if at the moment you have trouble remembering your dreams. They might not, and probably won't, make much sense but over time the messages from your dreams will become clearer and you will find it easier to recall them. In the morning, you might not even remember that you penned a message to yourself until you read it, but after a while it will become second nature and a pattern will form, even if you write in code or symbols that your sleeping mind understands.

Instructing yourself to have memories come to you in your sleep can be useful. This can be as direct as you like; thinking about time periods, places, feelings, desires to explore, or whatever feels comfortable. Or use direct suggestion to yourself, Subconsciously: 'As I sleep please bring to my awareness memories from my past lives in my dreams'. Of course, you may prefer a different instruction; for example, 'Let me dream of the past', or something similar.

Another option is to meditate during the day and instruct or ask for dream memories, as the subconscious mind is happy when asked. Generally, when my clients have been regressed they often get more awareness during their dreams.

If you believe you are holding onto an emotion attached to your past, put your awareness there as you drift off and expect the answers you are seeking to come to you. You could try, if you like, focusing your thoughts on wherever you think you might have a past life memory you wish to retrieve, in a similar way to daydreaming except the intention is to fall asleep with the scenes from your inner movie mind playing.

A nifty little way to fall asleep, while thinking about the journey you wish to take, is to stare straight ahead. Of course it will be dark so you aren't actually looking at anything, just staring. After a while, you may notice that you can't quite tell if your eyes are open or closed or you might fall asleep before that happens. Before doing this, as with any other method, remind yourself that you are safe and that you are just observing while trusting that your own inner-healing mechanisms will work for you at all times.

13

Future Life Progression

Prediction is very difficult, especially about the future.
Niels Bohr

Possibility, Probability, Inevitability

We all know that by understanding our past we can enable freedom in the present to create a perfect future. How would it be though, if you could actually check out your future and, if something doesn't look like you want it to, use your innate abilities to change it?

What if you have an idea of a desired outcome – whether in your personal or professional life – but can't quite work out the route? Can you imagine looking forwards to one of your incarnations to come or to a time way in the future?

Past-life regression is a well-recognized therapeutic technique, but now becoming more popular, as awareness grows, is future-life progression. It was actually one of my clients who introduced me to the possibilities of exploring what is to come by asking to look into her future. About sixteen years ago she introduced me to the possibilities of future exploration by asking me to take her forwards in time for her check out whether a business idea, that involved moving to Spain, would turn out. When she said that she wanted to go forwards in time I suggested she visit a fortune teller or similar, but her reply was that if you can go back to past lives why then shouldn't we be able to go forward? I couldn't think of any answer other than, 'Why not, indeed!' So we did. It was an eye-opener and her progression in time revealed that she was on the right track and the outcome would be good. She did move her family to Spain and started the business that went on from success to success.

Many times, while I am progressing a client or a group is checking out what is to come, I smile to myself and inwardly thank her.

What it actually does or doesn't mean to go forwards in time depends on personal beliefs and your understanding of life on a cosmic and quantum level. Some people choose to go forwards in this life, others to future incarnations, and it is possible to progress a specific number of years. Does this mean that we don't have freewill? Is it set in stone so if you see something you don't like the look of you are expected to grin and bear it? No, I think we have a rough guide to our lives with ideas flowing towards and away from us and we decide which path we take. Except, often people struggle to believe they have choices and get stuck in a life they aren't enjoying, feeling unfulfilled or frustrated and dissatisfied; maybe repeating destructive actions, having bad relationships or unable to settle in a career that is meaningful to them.

Often, just by observing various future options, they become stronger and better able to make changes if they so desire. Recently, a client was very unhappy, believing his life was of no value as he flitted from one job to another. He thought, deep down, that he would like to help people but was unable to think of a way. We went forwards to later in this life, which was a continuation of now, where he saw himself old and grumpy. He was still unhappy and was miserable about the wasted potential. I suggested we throw all options to the wind so he could look at an alternative option. In this one, he described being in a beautiful room standing by a couch. I could immediately 'see' his future and knew he was waiting for a client to come to him. I waited for him to tune into what was happening and he slowly saw himself as a Reiki practitioner in a clinic. After watching this, while smiling and shaking his head in disbelief, he fully associated with it and felt the experience as if it was actually happening. At that moment, he changed and knew this was his proper path. Afterwards, he looked younger and brighter and looked forwards excitedly in his life.

I believe you can examine possibilities, knowing what you know now, but by looking at different future options you can move into a probable life that you choose. If you decide to repeat the same old and do nothing different, you remain on the path of inevitability which is fine if you are happy and successful but not so if you are not. The inevitable path is also an option when you have set your intention on your desired future.

Every action you have ever taken – each thought and all your wishes – have created you and your life as it is today. It, therefore, follows that you are constantly designing and shaping your future.

I believe that each of us, as individuals, are the most qualified people to look at our own futures with the information we already have in our mind and brain. We own our memories, whether they have already happened or are yet to come. Looking backwards and forwards is a cathartic experience that gives many the feeling of completeness and being 'rounded'.

In the summer of July 2005, I received a call from a TV production company inviting me to take part in a program about looking into the future. My role was to progress a couple of people, which I duly did in my garden. To give it televisual appeal, they brought along a Klingon and, as you have probably surmised, this was a surreal experience. The phone call from one of the crew – saying, 'I'll see you later. I'm just off to Luton to collect the Klingon.' – remains in my mind as one of the strangest conversations ever. Anyway, back to the filming; I progressed two people who hadn't met and whose paths didn't cross, yet they relayed very similar experiences of future incarnations. All the tales from the future were very ordinary – even the Klingon's. This was sad for the director, as he was desperate to have a report on space travel and robots. It showed me that however much we wish for life to become a science fiction film, it will be what it will be. That afternoon is still talked about in the village and described as, 'when the Klingon came'.

Some years ago, Andrea experienced a regression and progression for a magazine feature with me. In her past life she was a patient in a mental hospital recovering from a breakdown and described the hospital and her feelings. They were mostly of a helpless resignation. We then worked our way forward in her current life and she visited her son's wedding. To finish, Andrea went to a future life where she found herself working as a brain surgeon, or, in her words, doctor of the head, with the name of Doctor Blake. At the time of the progression she/he was aged in the mid-forties and on a ward round. The post carried, or will carry if we're being pedantic, a lot of responsibility. From one to another, the contrast was clear. She felt helpless in the past and then moved on to being strong with many responsibilities, taking care of those with vulnerabilities. Andrea was able to 'chat' with Doctor Blake and get some advice for her present Self. Coincidentally, if there is such a thing, in this life she is interested in everything relating to the head and healing. Did her past trigger the route to her doctor persona via her fascination with psychology, or is it a metaphor of extremes? Does it matter?

Afterwards she said,

I think having the session and delving into my past life gave me an incredible insight into what was going on for me in this life now. What was most significant was the feeling I experienced when I could do nothing but let go of control within the past life, and because of where I was – in a sanatorium for the insane – I had to allow things to happen without my control or permission. Going on to then visit a future life as a brain surgeon was the natural next step and I felt back in control. I was reminded that I am my own person with the strength to do as I desire. In my life now I've always been keen to learn about

anything related to the head – psychology, behavior, communication – and I think this has really helped me now in terms of
allowing myself to go with the flow of life more: following my
creative instincts and deeper passions.

I have worked with clients who have a clear idea of what they
desire but can't see the wood for the trees. They have blockages,
obstacles, money issues, relationship problems and so on. The
usual pattern is they travel forward to 'see' their dream or plan
play out to them and from that point in the future they are able
to look back to the now to discover how to get there. The
responses from this are often things like, 'Well, I didn't expect
that', or 'Now, I know it is so obvious'. We tend to be our own
enemy when we create hurdles, and the moment we remove or
solve one we immediately create a new one. By going to the
outcome we can then allow ourselves to flow towards it and if,
on the way, there is hardship, heartache or a struggle we know
we will overcome it all and succeed. And, when we are truly in
the flow, the struggles stop; you no longer feel as though you are
banging your head against a wall and you can be free to enjoy
the experiences and fruits of your planting.

Here is a meditation script to visit your own future. You can
read it and then carry it out, record it or have someone else read
it to you.

Trust that your subconscious mind will show you a useful
moment or event in time. Or, if you are seeking something in
particular, think of it as you make yourself comfortable where
you will be undisturbed. It is up to you how you observe the
experience: whether fully in your future self to see it all
happening through your own eyes or in a detached way as a
viewer watching yourself.

Say to yourself, 'I welcome the opportunity to visit my
future'. At this point, if you like, you can determine how far.

Allow your breathing to be naturally regular, while you let
yourself become a little more relaxed each time you breathe out.

If you like, use an earlier meditation and deepener to relax or go straight in. As always, it is your choice.

Imagine you are in the hall of a castle, feeling safe and welcome, about to go up a stone stairway. Explore your environment and really get a feel for the place. It may well seem familiar to you. As you go up the stairs, hear the sound of your feet and notice the feeling of calmness as you move higher. When you get to the top, there are several doors and you are drawn to one in particular that you know is the 'Library of All'.

Go through the door and take in your surroundings.

On the far side of the library is a large table. Go now and sit at that table. Become aware of a book opened out in front of you – this is the book of you; it contains your past, your now and the book is open for you to see into your own future. Spend a few moments getting comfortable so that you may lose yourself in your dream of you. Gaze into the book and drift into the images and thoughts that float to your mind... It is like you are watching a film with you as the star, as a casual observer of your own future.

Watch it unfolding without judgment while making a mental note of anything you choose to remember and know that this is the life you are creating. Think of your dreams, plans and goals and trust that you can create your desires as you build a template for you – for your success, health, well-being and happiness. Add anything here that you think is pertinent to you.

Relax in this meditation until you are ready to awaken. As you bring yourself fully awake, you might like to make a few notes as triggers to remember more or help you make choices now and then.

You can vary the meditation by deciding how far in time to travel, or to what outcome. You can see what might happen in a given situation if nothing is changed and compare it to what might happen with very subtle shifts. You can even invent an outcome and see it in your future as if it has happened and then look back to the now for a path towards it.

Another way to visit your future is to meditate and be on a footpath. When you get to the direction sign, you can choose where to go. The sign can display whatever you like: a number of years, an outcome you wish to explore or the 'feeling lucky' one like a Google search.

You can even just jump forwards in time, as in, 'Subconscious take me to the year...' Or, 'I am now exploring my next life'.

Our mind is unable to differentiate imagination from reality and so by thinking 'as if', we set off a new course with different energies that allow us to be in a different 'flow'. This process is used a lot by my clients who are nervous about something, like an interview, exam or a performance. I ask them to show me 'as if' it is perfect and, when they fully experience it, a fantastic template is created in their mind. This shifts the energy flow into a positive one that they then step into to reap the benefits.

Please remember that you have created your life until this moment, so make sure the rest of it is fashioned as you truly desire.

Here are a couple of examples of future life progressions:

Jackie felt trapped in a relationship hurtling towards marriage and was afraid to back out for fear of upsetting any one or being embarrassed. She looked at a few possible futures: one where they drifted on making do and putting up with it all and another where she was alone but looking miserable. The third caused one of those mind boggling moments of confusion when she saw herself and her partner both married to other people but running a very successful business together. Unable to know quite what to do with this option, they both came to see me and we talked it through.

They were really fond of each other, but when they put on their honesty heads they admitted it was like a brother/sister relationship rather than a husband and wife one. Because they were so close and comfortable with each other, it made sense that they would succeed in business: something they had discussed but never pursued as they didn't want to be married to each other and share work. They hadn't ever really wanted to get married; it had happened around them and they had gone along with it as it was expected, and neither had been able to see a way out.

When they made the decision together to call a halt, they both felt relieved as if a huge weight had lifted, and happily left to plan the next step for their business.

This example shows how easy we can get sucked along a path or in life without really noticing what is occurring. So often I hear the words, 'I don't know how I've let myself end up here', or 'Is this in the script?' or 'Stop. I want to get off!' With marriages, one or both of the partners often knew it wasn't right but felt it had all gone too far to stop.

Paulo wanted to own a restaurant, but his friends and family constantly told him it was hard work, there was no money in it, long hours and so on. Despite this, he was really keen but didn't want to upset anyone by ignoring their advice. In the back of his mind was a little whisper saying, 'What if they're right?' that he found hard to ignore. He had a session with me to look forwards and try to silence the voice.

He only looked at one future: the one he really wanted, of his fantastic restaurant. He saw it full of customers and even two of his 'Doubting Thomas' friends were working in it, as was his mother. He discovered the little whisper in his head wasn't actually his; it was an accumulation of other peoples' worries on his behalf. He knew he was right and once he aired his intention a shift occurred and everyone became supportive. A couple of his friends, the ones he had seen in the progression, even invested in the project and became key players and partners. His mother's role was front of house and customers loved her.

When I first had dreams and premonition flashes of my future I didn't realize what was happening until I was immersed in the actual event. This is sometimes what happens when people get a déjà vu moment. Nowadays, I am able to tell, as I can notice the emotional charge and feelings, and you will too.

Are future life progressions showing you a possibility, probability or inevitability? Why not decide when you have looked for yourself?

14

Coincidences

Creativity comes from trust. Trust your instincts.
Rita Mae Brown

Serendipity or Cause and Effect

In the process of developing psychic abilities and intuition, it becomes clear that everything and everyone is connected by energy, thought and behaviors. The term 'synchronicity' was coined by Carl Jung, who described it as, 'temporally coincident occurrences of acausal events'. 'Acausal' meaning events occurring without cause and effect.

This blends beautifully with theories of parallel universes or quantum levels. This is a huge subject – maybe my next book? Jung felt synchronicity gave a good explanation of the collective unconscious giving order to what is seemingly chaos. How often have you had an idea, maybe regarding an invention, only for it to be created and developed by someone else? If you think back to the questions at the beginning of this book, about knowing what is going to happen, do many of the outcomes seem like amazing coincidences? Is coincidence another way to describe expected creation?

If we think about living in the flow or feeling the vibes, these terms also suggest everything and everyone is linked or connected. Examples of it in action are: you think of someone you haven't heard of for years and suddenly they call you or you are on the other side of the world chatting with someone in a queue and discover they are related to your neighbors.

Most of us have stories of our own regarding things that have happened that make us go 'wow' and think for a moment 'that was spooky'.

The following people have been kind enough to share their stories:

Ewa Griffiths, Hypnotherapist and Soap Creator.

A while back, when I was still doing my day job and trying to figure out how to divide my time between hypnotherapy and soap making instead of front-line work at a local council, the following wonderful moment happened:

Calling a random ticket number for a customer to see me, while dealing with his enquiry, he mentioned that he had recently moved to Kent, so I chatted away about how lovely I think it is there, etc., and asked where exactly he had moved. When he said that he was the new owner of a garden centre, farm shop and restaurant near Sissinghurst, I replied that I'd pop in for lunch some day soon, since at that time I was planning to do the farmers market at the castle. He asked what I was selling, so told him all about my wonderful soap, to which he said, 'Funny you should say that, we were just saying this morning, we really should have some handmade soap in our shop'.

Not only that – when I arrived at the lovely shop with all my soap (yes, they bought), there was also a therapy room for hire – in the most peaceful setting I could have hoped for – and a teepee in the field for workshops, and an indoor room for the same.

I'm in the habit of visualizing what I want my reality to look like, but not even my imagination stretched as far as 'and a shop to sell my soap, and oh, let's have a therapy room there as well'. Now all I have to do is remove remaining limitations to visualizations... It's all possible!

Deborah Wells, Author and Publisher.

When I left school I had no idea what I wanted to do, so I

floated around doing different jobs for a few years before training to be a registered nurse. On the first day I knew I had made a mistake! This wasn't the career for me. However, I stuck at it (just), and three years later I sat my finals.

However, even with finals looming, I just couldn't bring myself to revise – even though deep down I knew I had to finish what I started before I could leave (all I really wanted was to start my family). So the day before my finals saw me sitting in a deckchair in our back garden on a beautiful, hot June day. My book was lying closed on the floor beside me. And I knew I should be cramming like mad because there was so much stuff (most of the syllabus in fact) that I hadn't revised.

At the time, we lived on a hill that gave us fantastic views of the surrounding countryside. There was nothing around me but the farm up the road, and everything was absolutely still. There wasn't a breath of air around. Then all of a sudden, from absolutely nowhere, a strong breeze appeared. It was so strong it opened the cover of my 1000+ page hardback textbook. I was so disconcerted, I froze. The only bit of me that moved was my eyes as I watched, somewhat incredulously, as the pages leaved open. Then, as suddenly as the wind began it stopped, and I remember clearing my throat and cautiously peeping to see what page the textbook had opened on. It was page 654: Thyroid Surgery.

Again, I remember thinking that I should maybe revise this subject (I still own the book [*Watson's Medical-Surgical Nursing and Related Physiology*, 1987] and these pages still have the red highlights on them). Anyway, the next day when I turned over the exam paper I just grinned when, you guessed it, thyroid surgery was one of the questions. In fact, the exam required us to answer three questions from a possible six or nine and, as it happened, I could only answer three of them! Without the wind incident I would have certainly failed my finals!

But the story continues, as about three or four years later I actually developed hyperthyroidism – I was only about twenty-five/six years old by then. Then, a few years later in 2001, I had to have my thyroid surgically removed. It was while I was under anesthetic having my thyroid removed that I had my (sort of) NDE, where I met Death. It was largely due to that experience that I changed direction and began the research which eventually became *The Dark Man*, published by O-Books.

There are many, many other 'coincidences' that I could have sent; they really do happen all the time. However, I chose this because parts of it are empirically verifiable, and even the bits of it that aren't happened 'outside' of me, i.e. they weren't hunches or things I could have somehow intuited or even engineered.

Michael Eardley, Author, Blogger and Granddad.

1. I worked in Birmingham in the 70s and went on a training course with colleagues from London. I made friends with a guy there and we stayed in touch for a while, but he left the company and we lost contact.

Thirty years later, the first time I had been in London for over twenty years, I literally bumped into him coming out of Victoria Tube Station, one of the busiest spots in teeming London with hundreds of thousands of people milling about. Why him? Why there? Why didn't I collide with someone else when there were so many people? The mathematical odds on that have to be astronomical.

2. As a teenager we toured Europe with one of our older friends who was car crazy. He wanted to drive the Route of the Monte Carlo Rally through the Alpes Maritimes, so we did (phew, those hairpins!) and ended up in Monaco. Parking up in the hotel car park, we pulled alongside a car which

belonged to our driver's next door neighbor. Neither knew the other was making the trip.

I don't believe in coincidence.

Serendipity – Miracle at Midnight. Jacqui Metcalf, Writer and Psychic Medium

Arriving on a bitterly cold night, we flew into Manchester Airport tired and a little fractious after enduring an annoyingly delayed flight, coupled with the disappointment of having to come back home to a bleak and misty England after our happy holiday spent in the sun blessed island of Majorca.

Our little family struggled with heavy suitcases, trudging through the cold night air to reach the icy metal of our car: left alone and forlorn two weeks ago in the gloom of the concrete carbuncle, which served as the airport's isolated high-rise car park. The structure seemed eerily silent as only two or three similarly weary travelers made their way to their cars, gratefully setting off on their homeward journeys. Looking forward to the promise of a night's sleep in pristine, warm beds, three little children and two weary adults threw their luggage into the back of the car and pushed the key into the ignition, praying that the engine would roar into life on the first turn.

After several manic twists of the key with no sound of the engine forthcoming, we realized, on turning to see the expectant faces of our children, that the back reading light had been switched on and left for the entire duration of our holiday. Two weeks of this gently glowing aura left the car with no energy in its battery to drive us safely home to our welcoming beds. We tried to push the car along the darkened edifice of the building, but at every level that we became nearer to the exit, no splutter of the engine would be heard. We looked hopelessly around what seemed a vast terrain of emptiness. Could this really be Manchester at midnight?

Here we were stranded, cold and far from home with no telephone box (for this was the time before the mobile was thrust upon us) or a friendly, helpful motorist in sight.

Out of sheer fear and frustration, Ray viciously kicked the wheels of our now-defunct car and shouted for all the world to hear (except, it would seem, Manchester), and the cry of 'Jesus Christ!' rang out into the night sky. Perhaps blasphemy wasn't his best course of action for our problem, for as we looked heavenward, praying for something akin to divine inspiration, the portentous clouds seem to part, filling the skies with a soft but insistent falling of snow, which only served to complete our abject misery.

Our eyes fell away from the dark snowy skies, once more to gaze forlornly on our inert engine and its tiny occupants, now huddled together for warmth and safety.

And there, standing next to us, with a cheery smile and shiny van, looking for all the world like a knight with his shiny armor and trusty steed, was the wonderful apparition of an AA man, who appeared to be asking his time honored question of, 'Can I be of assistance, sir?'

We stood mute, open mouthed, afraid our knight of the road (and car park) would disappear as quickly and mysteriously as he seemed to materialize.

We fell silently back and let our Miracle at Midnight carry out the work for which he was ordained. With a flourish of red and black jump leads attached to our once impotent battery, the roar of two powerful engines spluttered into joyous life. Speechless with gratitude and bewilderment, we offered our last crumpled £20 note to the figure in front of us. Not totally sure whether our extraordinary mechanic was incarnate man or angelic visitor, he was without doubt a Godsend.

As we pulled away from the car park, we looked back once more to wave a grateful goodbye. It could have been the flurries of snow in the darkened skies obscuring our view, but it appeared that both our savior and his shiny armor had vanished silently into the night. Leaving us bewildered at our otherworldly experience, we drove silently and speedily on our road ahead.

What do these stories mean? Were they all coincidences or were the events and experiences created by the thoughts, feelings and actions of those concerned or involved?

Whatever is happening at any given moment affects everything else, so when we tune into the energy of events we become part of them. If you ask anyone about coincidences they will have a story to share. They are happening all the time. Some people will say there is no such thing, as there is a reason for everything and all the while we are creating our lives, behaviors and actions that affect those around us. Their behavior, in turn, affects those that they interact with and so on. We really are connected and in tune with everyone.

One of my own favorite coincidences happened this year. I was looking for a clinic to work in and had been for a few years. I visited several and met many lovely people, but none of them were quite right. I wanted to be in a beautiful peaceful building with other therapists. It was important that it was comfortable and preferably an old building rather than a new modern design.

I asked my friend, Moira, who works at the local paper, and therefore knows everyone, for some ideas. She said she could only think of one place that would suit me and it was called Pure, run by a girl called Charlotte Robins.

I called and left a message and when she returned my call (and left a message) she said she was sure we knew each other. We eventually managed to speak and meet and discovered we had actually worked together about seventeen years ago at a dance studio in the town where I did an occasional clinic. She had even had a session of hypnotherapy with me all those years before for driving test nerves. We slipped into friendship so easily and I am happily ensconced at Pure, which just so happens to be one of the oldest buildings in Alton.

And, oh yes she passed her driving test.

15

Law Of Cosmic Attraction

One must not lose desires. They are mighty stimulants to creativeness, to love, and to long life.
Alexander A. Bogomoletz

Law of attraction, cosmic ordering, wishful thinking, cause and effect, self-fulfilling prophesy, goal-setting and some might say prayer all describe the process of 'we get what we focus on'.

The theory of personal beliefs and attitudes affecting personal success was made famous by Napolean Hill in his book, *Think and Grow Rich*. One of his best known quotes: 'What the mind of man can conceive and believe, it can achieve'.

In 1908, Hill interviewed Andrew Carnegie, who, himself, believed that success was dependent on attitude. Together, after Hill's research and interviews with many entrepreneurs, they published *The Law of Success* as a study course. Carnegie made and gave away millions of dollars.

The same but updated version of these thoughts was reawakened by Barbel Mohr who created her book *Cosmic Ordering* in 1998 and who Noel Edmonds happily says is the reason behind his re-emergence into a successful TV career. From being dismissed by some as new-age fluff, many now live their lives with the belief of 'what you think is what you get'.

Historically of course, we have all been living with the knowledge and we know that we reap what we sow, but few of us have given thought to what any of it actually means. Many of my clients struggle to believe they have control over their life, but when we start to reduce the process of day to day living into bite-sized nuggets of information, it dawns in that delicious way of 'getting it'.

People tend to seek out the process of ordering from the Cosmos when they are feeling stuck or, more often, they are feeling cash poor. Something interesting I have observed is the connection between cosmic success, coincidence and serendipity. About four years ago my husband treated the whole family to a Greek holiday, nine of us, including Vinnie who was just a few months old. A couple of days before, Mick said he thought we should get a smaller buggy for Vinnie that would be easier to travel with on planes and boats. I looked in Argos and there was one for £70, so we planned to get it the day before we went, which would be the Thursday. On the Wednesday, Charlie and I were holiday shopping and I was queuing in the post office while she loaded the car. Suddenly, my mobile rang and it was a furious Charlie. A bird had pooped on her boobs while she was putting Vinnie in the car. She wasn't happy! I was unable to be sympathetic as I was too busy laughing, but consoled her by saying it was lucky and we should get a lottery ticket on the way home.

We did and I thought no more of it until the following day when squeals of delight rang through the house, as we discovered we had four numbers correct. We won £71 which equated to the buggy and my original pound returned. I hadn't wished to win the lottery to buy a buggy – my thoughts had been, 'I'll get cash to buy the buggy'. That was it. Coincidence? Maybe. Luck? Maybe. Did I order it with my thought? Maybe. The fact was we had a nice new buggy and the money I would have spent bought us all a very nice Greek lunch.

So, what is cosmic ordering and why should we get what we want? I think one of the best explanations and methods is the one shared by Helene Hadsell. In 1958, a very good year, she read *The Power of Positive Thinking*, by Dr. Norman Vincent Peale and put the premise into action and began to win things in competitions. She won prizes, such as holidays, cars, furniture and a house, among many others. She sums up positive thinking as, 'Picture the thing you desire as having already happened or taken place.' Her belief is that you can bend time and project your desired outcome into your future.

Helene describes her process as SPEC:

S – Select it by knowing clearly what you want.
P – Project it by seeing it as though it has happened or you have it.
E – Expect it by believing it is already yours.
C – Collect it by being ready to receive it.

Select, project, expect, collect. An easy formula that really does work. The problem some people come across is being unclear in their desires, thinking it's silly, believing they are not worthy or not being receptive to collection.

Therapists have been using the methods for years to assist clients into being well or making changes, i.e. imagine yourself as a non-smoker. Some can manage easily while others can't believe they can survive and so the perceived pain of giving up cigarettes over-rides everything else.

Cosmic ordering can have the same result. The orderer can't think of how life might be if they're not scrimping and penny counting, so these are the thoughts that stay strong and this is the mind-set they remain in. Or, they don't think they are worthy of love and, as all their previous relationships have turned sour, this is their start point and is the behavior that keeps being repeated.

Being unclear is another problem. An example is when you ask someone what they want and they say, 'I want to be successful'. What does that mean? It means different thing to different people. Some might equate success with money or fame. Some might equate it with raising a family. The mind might equate it with successfully crossing a road or brewing a nice pot of tea.

There are many tools for helping you to be clear and focused. Vision boards work by creating a board or part of a wall devoted to images of things that represent success. Whether that is houses, cars, piles of money, pictures of flowers, children healthy and happy or whatever is right for you. This will instill the positivity necessary to allow your desires to be created.

Another method is to make a vision-film with upbeat music to accompany it. Most computers have programs that make it easy to create a photo album that moves through the pictures in time with the music.

There are those who think wishing for material things is bad and that we shouldn't be so shallow. These are the same people who think healers and therapists should work for free as they have a 'gift'. My reply is that whether we like it or not we live in a material world and being solvent reduces nearly all the stress that people suffer. I say 'nearly' because there are many very rich people who are still miserable or stressed. Imagine having plenty of money for your life and then some; imagine having enough for you and your family and then the remainder can be gifted to those in need or donated to causes close to your heart. That's a good thought and feeling isn't it?

Attitude to money is a big issue with a gamut of emotions attached to it. If you hate paying bills or credit cards you are blocking your flow of money energy. I love settling bills and thank Mr Visa for the arrangement we have that lets me buy things when I choose on the understanding that I pay him what I owe. I know people who groan and moan about their bills, forgetting that they are already enjoying the pleasure of their purchases and ignoring the fact that if they don't pay they are actually stealing. This is another block created.

When we think about what we want, if we feel the emotion attached to the thought, the mind and body become excited and a surge of energy is created that propels us to our desire. If you want to write a wish list, do so. If you want to sit cross-legged chanting 'Mercedes', do so. If you want to post stick-its around your house with drawings of your selections, do so. Whatever works for you is right.

Okay, so you've decided what you'd like and created an image in your mind with or without the added aids. Now is the time to play 'as if'. How would you be if you had actually got your wish? Excited, happy, grateful?

We must add in here that gratitude is a good habit to have. Whatever you have got now, even if you are lacking, be grateful. If you are cross with your life, guess what? Yes, you will remain stuck and it is like wading through life's treacle. Some like to list their gratitudes each day – big or small. You can be grateful for the love of your family and the delicious cup of tea you just had. When you are grateful you are not needy. Is that a groan I hear? Are you thinking if I wasn't needy I wouldn't need cosmic ordering? Being needy creates just that, more and more need.

Being contented and happy clears the way for you to have and collect your selection. The art of positive thinking has been proven to help with reaching goals. Barbara Fredrickson, University of North Carolina, has the theory of 'broaden and build' – happiness and positive states of mind improve cognitive capacities. This allows us to build resources and see the big picture. Compare this to negativity and the narrow view of looking at things. Think of those who say, 'I'm never lucky. I never win anything. All my relationships fail'. We are exactly what it says on our tins.

Ready? Now then to collect? You've selected, projected and expected, so please accept what comes. My classic example is the meditation I did before I wrote my first book. I relaxed into the experience and imagined a beautiful summer day with people walking about holding a book. The sun was shining very brightly and made everything glow yellow. I liked that and made it stronger and clearer. Within minutes of finishing and still feeling warm and glowy, my phone rang. It was someone looking to hire distributors of the Yellow Pages. I almost wept as I said to the poor confused woman on the other end of the phone, 'No! That's not it'.

However, it was exactly it. I hadn't specified my book. I had just seen lots of yellow books with many people looking at them. I couldn't have been more precise about offering myself to deliver phone directories.

If this is all seems too much for you, try starting off by using this successful technique to release, create or reap whatever you desire by writing your own life in the form of a story. You don't have to literally write it: imagining it or recording are perfect methods. Create your story, beginning wherever you wish: in this life or a past one. Pretend it is the exact set of events and circumstances that you would love. If it is in the past, gather up all the learning toward whatever you need to benefit your life now. Imagine you have the knowledge necessary for your perfect life of bliss, and design the future of your choice.

You can do this as often as you like, changing, tweaking or rewriting as you go. It's your life, your story, you have control. The beauty of being in charge of yourself is that, if you change an emotional hold from a stress-filled one to a happy one, the mind will change your physiology and you will feel different.

As you design your life, you will automatically be giving yourself ideas, affirmations and suggestions of success and abundance. Because you've cleared away anything at all that might be in the way, physically, mentally, spiritually or metaphorically, it will become your reality. And, if you don't like it, you can change it.

If you find this chapter difficult, may I suggest you go back and check your chakras in case you are holding onto stress that is subconsciously sabotaging your progress or success with your orders.

Another point to mention is that lots of people expect things to turn sour as soon as they experience good things. Many live in dualism: good and evil, dark and light, happiness and misery. They think it is somehow wrong to have too much pleasure or happiness, so wait, while brooding on and creating negative experiences. When they have manifested this they reward themselves in their cleverness and knowing. Please don't let the made-up guilt of success get in your way. Why not balance success with gratitude or abundance with sharing?

The last word goes to Henry Ford – 'Whether you think you can or whether you think you can't, you're right'.

16

Psychic Readings

If this is coffee, please bring me some tea; but if this is tea, please bring me some coffee.
Abraham Lincoln

At the salons we might read each other but this is as much to determine how we operate as it is to understand or help another.

If you have a volunteer, you can have a go at giving a reading. Most people are up for it as it can help them think something through or enable them make a decision on something. If it fits with your beliefs, ask your guide and angel to be present and imagine the room and yourselves bathed in white light.

Ensure the person you are reading for is comfortable while you take a few calming breaths into a light, meditative, focused state. If you breathe at the same rate as them they too will relax and you'll sink to the same level. Do this by matching their breathing and then gently slow your down and theirs will too. You are going to scan them on a psychic level. Begin to tune into them first by observing their aura and then their chakras. Should you get the urge to ask questions, do so, and if you receive information, share the things you feel are right. Honesty is usually the best policy, but if you detect something not so good diplomacy is called for. It wouldn't be particularly nice to be on the receiving end of, 'Your husband is having an affair and is about to leave you, but don't worry you'll be dead in three weeks'. I have made this extreme to make a point. When you work on a psychic level you may be privy to very personal and private things. If you can't honor the person's privacy, please do not proceed.

A simple comment such as, 'I'm detecting a little tightness in your neck', may bring the response that the person is tense or worried about something and you can take it from there. It isn't your job to sort out their world as this is about sharing and, if necessary and if wanted, healing.

Perhaps your 'client' is after specific information and, if this is the case, ask them to focus on their question or the subject they want to know about. All you need do is allow thoughts, images or guidance to flow through you to them. You are merely the channel, but if you get a light pinging in your head as a solution, you can say, 'I'm wondering if... (e.g. a chat with a particular person, seeing a doctor, having a swim, massage or so on) ...might be useful', or something similar. Make it clear that you are not diagnosing or prescribing; you are merely a guide. When things don't seem to make sense, share them anyway, as it is up to the receiver to determine whether the information is useful.

The reality of all this is that the client has the information and usually knows the answers but sometimes muddlement takes over and all they need is a little help with their inner filing and sorting. If they ask you a question that you don't get an answer to, please say so. Lying or making stuff up will come back to bite you, so best you don't go there ever. Trust your intuition and the guidance you receive and you'll both benefit hugely.

Barnum

I'll do a quick reading on you now.

You are trustworthy and honest with a knack to know exactly the needs of others. People are attracted to you and admire you. You have a tendency to sometimes be critical of yourself. You are very intuitive but don't always trust your instant reactions only to be proved right.

You have a great deal of unused capacity, which you have not turned to your advantage. You prefer a certain amount of change and variety, and become dissatisfied when hemmed in by restrictions and limitations.

You pride myself as an independent thinker, and don't accept others' statements without satisfactory proof.

You have found it unwise to be too frank in revealing yourself to others.

At times you are extroverted, affable and sociable, while at other times you are introverted, wary and reserved.

There, have I got some of them right? These sentences are called Barnum statements. They are generalizations that we can make fit to ourselves so we believe them to be personal. They are the tools of the cold-reader but, having said that, they can apply and be useful to get in the flow when reading someone. Deep down most people are kind gentle souls, but their life experiences might have made them jaded or miserable. It is perfectly acceptable to remind them of all their good points.

You might find you have a knack for readings of a particular kind or you may prefer to have a few things you check and share. Usually, a reader looks at health, career, finances and relationships.

Relationships can be a problem for many as they seek 'the one' and you can help them a lot by sharing how to be free from old programs they are running that might be hindering or blocking them. If they say they are looking for their soul-mate, remind them that soul-mates aren't necessarily the sources of all pleasure and often they are in their lives to challenge or teach a valuable life lesson.

Decide firstly what you are reading for and then scan the other person in the way you feel most comfortable. When you begin, first reading by looking for answers relating to each chakra, you can open your intuitive reading channels and free up the other person of any negativity they might be holding. A chakra reading, as well as other kinds, can be done remotely as it is the energy you are looking at or sensing. Checking out auras; again in person or remotely will also tell you a lot. You really don't need to tell them everything you are detecting. So, for example, 'Ah, you have a ball of muckiness attached to your heart. This means you are hurting in love or your have a health issue', is not the best method.

Instead, 'Would you like to discuss your feelings?' is a better approach.

Before any reading it is important that you are free from your own issues and judgments, so begin by taking a couple of cleansing breaths and centre yourself by putting your energy in your solar plexus and allowing it to flow around you for protection. When you are stilled internally, scan yourself to check for any tensions and if you find any breathe them away or mentally massage them free. If you have begun working with your guide or angels, ask them to assist you; otherwise, from here tune into the person who is seeking the reading.

Now, while to begin with all this sounds and seems fun it can cause surprises, particularly when you discover how good you are. Please be humble in that you are receiving privileged information that you have accessed from someone's psyche: you cannot walk on water and you are not the answer to everything.

So often in this line of work, therapists and readers get delusional with ideas of having a God-like power. This is followed by arrogance and the unwavering ability to sound like a prize numptie or patronizing idiot. These people then tend to spout rubbish as their own ideas, and judgments cloud the way for authenticity and they are unable to get any true information, so they make it up. When the person on the receiving end then says something like, 'This isn't meaning anything', they get the reply, 'Oh, it will, trust me!' and then they throw in a few Barnum statements. That noise in the background is me growling.

For some starting off giving readings, they discover they can tune into the person's past lives and get what seems like a movie playing in their heads. With this kind of reading it is usually the emotional attachment to a memory that needs to be released and this is done by sharing what you receive and then gently working through whatever comes. Often, just the acknowledgment is the release, but sometimes a little more is needed.

Whatever kind of reading you do, if you detect illness, drug abuse or illegal happenings stop immediately and suggest they seek help elsewhere.

When the reading is over, make sure the person is okay and grounded and then make sure you are grounded and free from any debris that they might have dumped.

To begin this type of work can be invigorating and tiring, so take care to not overdo it and always ensure you have your own protection in place before and after. You do not want bits of anxiety energy looking for a new home and landing on you as a warm available host.

Keep in mind that you are not a doctor (unless you are) or the police (unless you are) or God (Hi there. Is that really you?!).

17

Psychic Fun

Always laugh when you can. It is cheap medicine.
Lord Byron

If you have created, or wish to form, a psychic circle of friends to work with while you all develop your talents, here are some fun things to try.

ESP

Zener Cards were created in the 1930s by Karl Zener for use in experiments with Joseph Banks Rhine, who coined the phrase 'Extra Sensory Perception', ESP. Mr. Rhine is usually referred to as J. B. Rhine.

A Zener pack is five sets of five different cards comprising of a circle, a Greek Cross, three wavy lines, a square and a five-pointed star.

To test for ESP, the participant says or writes down what they intuit the next card to be. This is best done quickly and for them to not be told until the end how many they got right. Of course it is also possible to test yourself by saying what you think the card will be before you turn it over.

To test telepathy or clairvoyance, someone focuses on each card in turn and 'sends' the image to a/some receiver/s. This can be fun as there are those who are brilliant at sending while others are better at receiving. A few can do both.

Another ESP test is for you to put different pictures in envelopes and have others guess what they are before being opened. At a retreat a few years ago, I did this and one girl laughed the second I gave out the envelopes, as she could hear a song in her head to accompany the picture. Now, I had packaged these at home before I went to the venue and they were with me until I shared them. The idea was for each participant to have the envelope with them throughout the weekend and then at the end of the retreat everyone shared their thoughts. The hits were amazing. Although not always 100% exact, the results were mostly spot on. The ones that were slightly off were still close; if the picture was a building, the shape was invariably described in detail if not the actual name of the building. The London Eye was described as a circle or funfair wheel and the pyramids as geometric shapes.

Anyway, back to the girl who heard the song; she said with unwavering confidence before she opened her envelope, 'I knew the second I held it, it is a picture of Sooty', and she was correct. Her insight allowed her to intuit the picture from inside the envelope: not from me; I had no idea what picture was in each one, as they were all the same with no markings.

Remote Viewing

In the world of spies and spooks, tales abound of remote viewing but in our little circle we are just playing! There are a few different ways to get started, so to begin with have someone put an object in a building or location. Then, either they tell you what the object is and you take your mind to locate it, or they tell you where it is hidden and you use your mind to discover the object. Another way is to have someone draw a picture in one room while someone else 'views' with their mind what it is.

Remote viewing is best done in a gentle state of calm and you might be the type who prefers to just take yourself off on a journey in your mind to explore somewhere or to check out someone you know and who is happy for you to 'visit'. Can you remember earlier my client looking at his home and seeing his flat mate arrive back earlier than expected? That is what he did. If you have an agreeable friend, you can ask them to do something at a particular time and you tune into them and attempt to see and then describe what they are going. If you are working in a psychic group or circle, you can take turns by using different actions or have some hide an object and the rest of the group use their remote viewing powers to locate it. I have put something on the shelf in my office above my computer. It is directly in front of the silver box. Can you see what it is? The answer is on my website.

Playing cards can be good for trying out remote viewing, and as people get better they will even be able to 'see' what the card is. Mind boggling eh?

Location Dowsing

You might prefer to dowse to find a hidden object rather than view remotely. You could start with a drawing of your house and have someone hide an object that you then dowse for over the picture. As you progress, you can locate objects or people using ordnance survey maps. Personally, I think this is the same as remote viewing but without the ritual and the pendulum as the tool to show the exact spot. You can use your pendulum in exactly the same way as before by holding it over the drawing or map and asking it to show you a positive movement when it is over the right spot, or if you have one with a point it can direct itself and land on the map's location. Be prepared, though, because this might make you jump when it feels like the pendulum has a life force of its own as it launches.

Spells

Ooh! Too spooky? Not at all. A spell is a creation through intention. It is not something conjured by an old hag over a cauldron full of body parts and if you try to insist I will deny it every time! Spells can be performed simply by focusing on a desire or outcome with a clear mind or they can be elaborate with ritual, the calling on of elements or worship to the gods and goddesses of your choice. You don't have to be or call yourself a witch to perform fantastic spells with outstanding results.

If you'd like to have a go at a ritual, try a gentle introduction using a candle, bowl of water, bowl of earth and a joss stick. Each of these is a representation of an element. You might like to make yourself an alter. This can be a table or shelf in a quiet area in your home or a stone in your garden and can be as fancy or as plain as you like. Put your equipment on it and quietly meditate in front of it, focusing on whatever you are creating. If, for example, you are sending healing or success wishes to someone, you can put their photo or a symbolic representation on your alter.

Some people create a very simple space with just a crystal or two and this is perfectly fine. When you have finished your spell, thank the elements for listening and helping to action your desires. If you feel silly don't worry that will pass and soon you will be an old hag – Whoops! Sorry, I mean 'old hand'! And, of course, if you wish to go sky clad and dance about in the moonlight just remember: don't do anything that might frighten the horses!

Sigils

The use of sigils are sometimes associated with darkness or black magic and, although some have been representations for badness (for example, a Nazi swastika is actually a reversed symbol of peace and good fortune), in my, and I hope your, world they are used for good. A sigil is a shape, drawing, picture or object that represents an affirmation, belief, spell or energy. They might also be called charms or amulets and there are many you will already be familiar with:

Cross – Jesus
Ankh – key of life

Pentagram – the elements
Signs of the Zodiac
Labyrinth
Yin Yang – male and female, balance

I'm sure you can think of many others, including reiki symbols. They too are sigils. When a sigil is created often an incantation or spell is chanted to infuse energy that will remain within it until time to be shared. Physical sigils are often used as in crossing fingers, making the sign of the cross or putting the thumb between first and second finger to denote a cross to ward off evil or bad fortune. The meditation pose with thumb and finger joined to form a circle represents unity and balance.

For your use, you can draw your own symbol on paper or in the air with a sweeping arm movement that represents something personal to you, or you can use a spoken acronym.

Think of what you want, e.g. happiness and health, and the spoken sigil will become 'hah'. You can chant or sign 'hah' repeatedly and it will act as a powerful affirmation and mind training technique. How about slim, sexy and successful? – 'sss' is a good noise to make. You can even use terms or words that are in use all the time that will trigger something in yourself every time you see or hear them. I'm thinking of 'BBC' as in bold, beautiful, calm or brilliance, bountiful, creative. Please create your own and have fun doing so.

The Magic Check

This is a powerful technique for freeing a negative attitude to money and can be an eye-opener to your own feelings associated with having lots, or not. Try doing it for one whole month. If you are in a group or circle it is fun to share your experiences with the others.

You begin on day one by writing yourself a check for £/$10, made out to you and signed from The Universe. On the second day, you double the amount, the third double again and so on. As you write each check, you also write what you are spending it on. The purpose is that you spend it on yourself and the things you want. Not what you need, but on your heart's desires and what you would get if money was no object and you had enough and then some. Extravagance rules in this game. After day twenty, you may write what you would like to buy for others. You may not write 'give it away' or donate to a good cause – be specific. This is all about the energy of money, and spending it – even on imaginary purchases – is a good way to charge (ha ha) it with power to ensure it flows back in abundance. It is important to really think about how you feel in your spending and I promise that if you have money issues or feel guilty about even imagined spending, by playing this game your inner connection with it will shift and you will switch to a state of receptivity.

Psychometry

Objects hold onto energy vibrations from their user or owner and there are people who can detect/sense this when they hold them. The energy is stored, it seems, in a similar way to how a tape records information. In a group, it is fun to each put something with personal meaning secretly into a container and then for everyone to take one object out and 'read' it. This is done by simply holding it and taking a couple of calming breaths to tune into the frequencies. The reader then says whatever they are experiencing without the owner claiming it until everyone has shared their own reading.

The energies can manifest as images, thoughts, feelings, the history of the object, sounds, tastes, smells or any combination of these. If the object belonged to someone else before the present owner, the reading might relate to another person or to the location of where the object was stored.

Another way is to work in pairs and to hold an object or

keepsake belonging to the partner and reading that way. This can often be more intimate and revealing. Without sounding too 'out there', I tend to think that the object only releases information when it is appropriate and sometimes it might need release from stagnated energies of grief or sorrow.

Buildings hold energy and I'm sure you've experienced that feeing of 'vibes' in a newly visited place, good and bad. Again, if a building has experienced sadness, misery or high energy (for example, a prison), this remains and resonates when you enter.

I often feel emotions stuck or attached to buildings; the most notable being Lanhydrock House in Bodmin. There we were, strolling about exploring the magnificence of the place, when suddenly I felt sick, hot and as if I was suffocating. It was so powerful, I thought the roof was coming down on me and I had to escape very quickly. By the time I got out I was shaking and felt like weeping. The house has a very sad history in that there was a devastating fire in 1881. The house was restored and refurbished, but it seems it still holds the memory of the sadness. I think most people detect in this way, but maybe just put it down to being tired or in a bad mood and don't recognize the connection or the trigger.

Group Energy Creation

One of the exercises I do in the Beyond Bliss retreat is to get everyone to write something positive, loving and wonderful for the world. People write all over an A board in any language, any direction and often embellish it with hearts and beautiful drawings.

Together we then focus our attention on the board and meditate together by synchronizing our breathing with everyone else. After a while, we imagine all the wonderful energy of the love and positivity in the room with us bathing and caressing our souls. From here, each participant imagines sharing this amazing energy, which by now has a huge momentum, with people they know and care for. This energy is then set free into the world to go wherever it would be of use.

The whole thing creates feelings of awe, sometimes accompanied by tears, but always thoroughly enjoyed.

18

Extra Meditation Scripts

Most folks are about as happy as they make up their minds to be.
Abraham Lincoln

All the meditations in this book can be changed or adapted in ways that you prefer – they are yours for you to do as you wish.

Here are a few meditations or creative visualizations. They can be used as stand alone exercises or after you have induced a lovely state of calm and inner peace. Before each one, centre and still yourself and then gently close your eyes.

Silver Liquid Light

Imagine that a beautiful healing silver liquid light is flowing into, over and through you from the top of your head down. With each gentle breath, sense, feel or imagine the light calming, soothing, cleansing, healing… doing whatever is necessary wherever it flows.

Allow it to slowly and rhythmically bathe you in comfort. As the liquid slowly travels down your body, feel the sensations of harmony and balance. Blissful waves of inner peace. When the liquid light flows down your arms and legs, imagine all stress dripping out of the ends of your fingers and toes… feeling loose and limp. Tranquil. Every cell in your whole being is resting in this healing, soothing, motivating energy.

Be in the liquid light for as long as you need or want. Feel rested, invigorated or a combination. This liquid will give you whatever you choose.

When you are ready to awaken, bring yourself gently alert.

Breathing Count

This is lovely and really helps with focus; plus, it will show you how easy it is for your mind to wander. Be comfortable and take a few still breaths. When you are ready, consciously slow your breathing very slightly and begin counting, but only on the out-breath.

In, out, one. In, out, two. In, out, three, and so on. If you can get to ten the first time you are doing very well. I know as you read this it seems easy, as surely it's just counting, but when you actually try it, it is a different matter. Don't put a number in your head to get to as it is best to work to time or until you reach a natural stop.

If you say I'm going to try and reach fifty it might add stress. The first few times I did this exercise I lost count or forgot after three or four, but now I find it much easier and sometimes use the technique to go to sleep.

Meditating in this way helps people who are left-brain dominant to relax, because it answers the need to be logical or sequential. When you are ready to awaken, bring yourself gently alert.

Opening Your Third Eye

This meditation will help you to switch on your intuition. You might have a similar experience when you do chakra work and focus on your brow.

Put your attention in the centre of your forehead and imagine you are looking out and back in through your third eye. As you relax into the experience, picture or imagine an eye just above your line of sight (as it would be if your eyes were open) looking at you. What color is it? What shape? Is it blinking? This eye is yours and you find you can direct the view the more you tune in and trust yourself. When you are fully aware, your intuition will be spot on.

If you like, you can take yourself on a journey and use the eye to observe wherever you are. If you are giving readings, your third eye can scan people inside and out to check their health and energy levels.

When you are ready to awaken, bring yourself gently alert.

Step into the Flow

Think about everything around you and imagine it all broken down into its smallest elements and vibrating in harmony with everything else. See the energy flow of everything towards and from everything else. See it as a beautiful shimmering flowing river that connects all. Step into the river and feel yourself flowing with it. This is the flow.

When you are in the flow everything seems brighter, better, stronger, calmer, more secure, more peaceful and more successful. When you are in the flow you experience more good 'luck'. You experience feelings of harmony and inner peace.

You can remain in the flow as the way to be all the time if you choose and I promise it is a lovely place to be.

Automatic Writing

This can be fun, occasionally scary and often an eye-opener. All that is needed is a pen and paper. You rest your pen on the paper and put yourself, or the group goes, into a light trance while saying something like, 'I am going to record my subconscious thoughts as they flow through me'.

You might find yourself doodling or scribbling, but maybe words will start to appear as your hand moves across the paper. My reference to it sometimes being scary is the speed that automatic writers can get to. After a while, you will naturally stop and you can look to see if you have a page of gobbledygook. This technique often alerts someone that they are a channeller of knowledge or a receiver and sharer.

Meeting the Sage

Imagine you are walking through a beautiful safe forest. The sunlight gently dapples through the trees and as you walk through the rays of light you feel calm and peaceful. You hear the sounds from the woods and if you like you can touch the trees and sense their strength and power.

A little way ahead is a small clearing and on the edge is a small wooden hut. There is someone in it or just by the door and you know you are there to meet the person. If the door is shut, knock and it will open and there in front of you is the Wise Sage. Feel a wave of unconditional love, and as you look into the sage's eyes notice the sensation of familiarity. You know this person but have forgotten. The Sage is putting something into your hand but don't look yet; just close your fingers around it. You may ask the Sage a question, anything you like and you will get a response. This will either be in words or in your mind, telepathically. When you have the answer say 'thank you' and leave. Know that the hut is gone as you walk away, but you feel wonderful. Before you reach the edge of the woods glance down at the gift in your hand, but know you might not immediately understand its meaning.

Take a few moments to assimilate your visit and then, when you are ready to awaken, bring yourself gently alert.

Candle Meditation

Light a candle of your choice. The idea is that you gaze into the flame, so please ensure it is in a safe place because it won't help your relaxation if you think it might fall. Lose yourself in the flame and allow your mind to wander in a free-flow way. Let yourself drift and you may find you slip into a trance-like state with your eyes remaining open, continuing to gaze but without seeing the flame. You might see two flames as your eyes relax and the flame may change color or seemingly dance for you. Just go fully with whatever you experience without any analysis or judgment until you are ready to awaken and then bring yourself gently alert.

Protection

Protecting yourself is a good habit to instigate before any psychic experiences, whether that is giving readings, leading or being part of meditations or group work. Think of a seed of power in the centre of your being beginning to grow and spread though you until you are full of the powerful energy that has grown. Let it travel through you until you are encased in the bubble it creates.

This protective bubble deflects all negativity away from you, but allows positivity in. You are safe in your bubble and you might like to start each day with this easy quick technique, especially while you are learning and experiencing many new things.

Grounding

At the end of every technique, exercise, meditation or psychic reading or healing session please make sure that you are fully grounded. Often, when people awaken their psychic and intuitive abilities, they complain of headaches or a woozy light-headed feeling, but grounding will prevent this happening. It is also why people are described as fluffy or airheads. It's because they are so up in the higher chakras they forget to be attached to the world.

Dancing, stamping, walking, running, doing housework, making tea all work, but it might not be practical to do any of these things, so imagine being a tree with the roots growing down through your back and legs into the earth where they fully support you. That's all you have to do. Simple, eh, but so overlooked.

19

The Psychic Circle

If it's the Psychic Network why do they need a phone number?
Robin Williams

There are some people who prefer to develop their psychic abilities in private without ever mentioning it to anyone else, just quietly getting on with it, but others like the thought of working in a group with like-minded souls. You might feel inclined to organize and lead a group or, if you have some friends interested, you can form a circle.

If you decide to host your own, you need to decide on the perfect location and put the word out. If you already have a group, generally each member takes a turn at hosting and decides on the venue or invites members to their home.

It tends to work best if you or the group decides on a format for each meeting with a different theme or subject each time.

Here is a template for meetings that you are welcome to follow:

Lighting a candle is a good opener followed by the welcome from the host, who shares what is up for discussion and how long the meeting will last. It is best to have a definite start and finish time. Of course, if people wish to stay longer and chat that is fine, but the actual meeting end time is fixed.

Set the rules – it is good to remind yourselves each time you meet.

1. Respect for each other at all times.
2. Privacy. Sometimes part of opening up psychically involves sharing thoughts and feelings. These must not be

discussed away from the group.

3. Care. Ensure any one being healed, read or worked on is cared for.
4. Positivity. Negativity can spoil the dynamics of a group.
5. Time for everyone. Do not let one person dominate the discussions.
6. Have fun.

Add you own.

Even if you are a close group of friends, I must emphasize the importance of rules to ensure you all have the same expectations. You'll be surprised at what can come out of the closet in intimate psychic circles! When the rules are shared, often by having them written down on a board or read out from a handout, move onto a cleansing opening meditation (see the end of the chapter). The host usually leads the meditation, but it might be that your group likes to share roles. So, one hosts, one leads the discussions or exercises; the speaker, one leads meditations, one is the time-keeper and so on. It can be fun to draw lots over who does what at each meet.

When everyone is focused, discuss how people have been or any experiences they wish to share from the previous session.

The next bit is the theme; for example, suppose in this session you are working on auras; the speaker can read from this book or from their own knowledge or research and a discussion follows. What are everyone's thoughts? What experiences have people already had? Plus anything else anyone wishes to share.

Move on then to the practical techniques or the meditation if that is needed, i.e. past- or future-life exploration.

Ensure everyone is grounded and have a break that usually includes a drink and nibbles.

After the break, chat about what everyone experienced and help each other, if necessary, to understand what did or didn't happen. Some people will love some of the exercises, while some won't. It might be that in one meeting everyone will love it and 'get it' but in another no one will and there'll be lots of head shaking and muttering. 'You can't please all of the people all of the time' is never truer than in psychic development. Usually, though, it is a mix of liking and not so and some things grow on you as you learn more and get different or better results.

When the discussion is over, plan the next meeting and if you are all going to do homework. It is best if the work continues between classes as it helps everyone with the tuning-in process.

Before the closing meditation, create a powerful bundle of group energy and send it to each other, to those you love and then out to the world.

End with the closing meditation, grounding and extinguishing the candle.

In all you have:

Lighting the candle
Welcome
Rules
Meditation
Catch-up
Theme
Break
Discussion
Plan next meeting
Group healing and energy to world
Meditation and grounding
Extinguish the candle

This is a guide, so feel free to chop and change. While psychic development is happening, you might like to keep a journal, grimoire, or some prefer to have a book of shadows: they're not just for witches, but you will soon find that your family members and friends, if they know what you are doing, will start to call them coven meetings. This can be your own private diary where you record your thoughts, experiences, dreams, goals, ideas, plus anything you think or feel is useful, or the group can have one, or both. In some groups, members like to bring their books to each meeting and read from them.

Enjoy your circle and grow together.

Opening Meditation

Sit comfortably, with your feet flat on the ground. Take a few slow breaths and allow all noise apart from an emergency to wash over you and relax you a little more.

(The following should be read rhythmically in time with the breathing).

Imagine drawing in relaxation from the ground into your feet as you breathe in and flow back down as you breathe out.

On the next breath, let the relaxation move into your ankles and then back down.

On the next breath, let the relaxation move into your calves and then back down.

On the next breath, let the relaxation move into your knees and then back down.

On the next breath, let the relaxation move into your thighs and then back down.

On the next breath, let the relaxation move into your hips and then back down.

On the next breath, let the relaxation move into your pelvis and then back down.

On the next breath, let the relaxation move into your lower back and then back down.

On the next breath, let the relaxation move into your tummy and then back down.

On the next breath, let the relaxation move into your middle back and then back down.

On the next breath, let the relaxation move into your chest and then back down.

On the next breath, let the relaxation move into your upper back and then back down.

On the next breath, let the relaxation move into your neck and then back down.

On the next breath, let the relaxation move into your shoulders and then back down.

On the next breath, let the relaxation move into your face and then back down.

On the next breath, let the relaxation move into your head and then back down.

All the way up from your feet to the top of your head can now rest and relax. Rest and relax.

I will now count from one to five and you can double you relaxation on each number.

One… Doubly relaxed.

Two… Doubly relaxed.

Three… Doubly relaxed.

Four… Doubly relaxed.

Five… Doubly relaxed.

Soothe away any tensions by mentally massaging them away and rest more and more with each gentle beat of your heart.

As we now open our circle, we are joining our knowledge together to work as one and for the good of all.

Rest in the place of comfort way down deep inside where all is well. Take a few moments to enjoy inner calm and, when you are ready, bring yourself awake.

Closing Meditation

Sit with your feet flat on the floor. Take a few calm breaths and sink inside to assimilate everything that has been discussed (allow a few minutes of quiet) and do your own inner filing. Tie up any loose ends that you sense.

Make sure your body and mind are clear and allow waves of inner peace to bathe you in comfort.

As we now close our circle, we keep everything safe while we continue to develop our abilities until we meet again. Draw energy down your body, through your feet and into the ground. Bring yourself awake and ensure you are fully grounded.

The final part is extinguishing the candle. That is the sign that the meeting is over.

If you are studying or developing alone, you might still like ritual in your lessons, but it isn't necessary and, if you don't like to, please don't think it is essential to achieve results. Once you start opening up your abilities, you can have experiences at any time, often out of the blue.

As always just go with the flow and enjoy whatever comes your way.

20

Living The Psychic Way Everyday

Everyone is born with psychic abilities. It's just a matter of knowing how to tap into it.
Mettie L.

Now you know all the various ways to awaken your psychic intuition you may be wondering how you can use them each day and even if you should. You will by now know which methods and techniques you prefer in the development of your psychic intuition and are probably already using some of them. Remember, you can switch things off if you are feeling bombarded or if you think things are moving too fast. Once you start to live in this, some might say, more spiritual way, new experiences might creep up on you most of the time. When you step into a different energy flow, you might be aware of changes in all areas of your life, from your health, moods and sleep pattern. You may have a desire to devour as much information as you can and want to take classes from as many different teachers as you can. You may also have the desire to share your own knowledge; if you have the urge to work as a light-worker then that is most likely your destiny; reading this book is not a coincidence but a demonstration that you are on the right path.

I could outline a daily to-do list for you to live the psychic way, but I think as a grown-up you can design your own life in the way that works for you and for you to reap your own successes. However, I will make a few suggestions to get you started, but you will soon find it all becomes second nature and you are probably already doing them to one degree or another.

Meditate – even a few minutes will make such a difference to your life that you will soon be unable to remember how you managed before. Your health will improve, as will your state of mind. Continuing with meditation practise will also ensure that your fine-tuning continues.

Give thanks – If you follow a religion, do this in your prayers. If you don't follow a specific path, be grateful for everything you have and thank whomever or whatever you choose. Thank yourself for being a beautiful person ready to be a light-worker. Thank those around you for being there. You don't have to do this out loud; if you think it might be uncomfortable for them do so in your prayers or meditations.

Share – If you have some of anything, share it. I don't mean inflict people with what you think they need; I mean make small donations to a charity – just pennies if that is all you can spare – or share your time by listening to people. If the old lady at the bus stop wants to tell you about Uncle Jim in the war, let her. Empty your cupboards of stuff you don't use and donate to charity shops. Think about what you can share and do so. You are not doing it to feel good but a by-product of this is that you actually will.

And, the more you share, the more will come back to you.

Help people – If you see someone struggling, offer help. It might be someone crossing a road, or a mummy in a pickle in the supermarket. Don't assume they can manage, but if they decline your offer so be it. Do not take it personally.

Accept – If someone pays you a compliment or gift, accept with grace. Don't do the whole, 'What this old thing?' or 'Oh, really? You shouldn't have'. Be gracious. If someone takes the time or trouble, the least you can do is accept.

Be in the Flow – What it says!

My Final Word
I have shared this short list to remind myself as well as you that when we are successful we can share it to create positive

energies in ourselves and to those around us. The benefit flow will grow exponentially and the more we all remember to do so the more we will all get.

My aim for this book was to have a fluff-free, to the point, how-to, because that is what my clients and those who come to my workshops and retreats asked for. I have written the book I wish I had read when I was having strange experiences and thinking I was the only one.

Living the Psychic Way is a philosophy for life and allows us all to live in the flow, trusting our vibes, allowing our sixth sense to blossom and all the other clichés that relate to psychic abilities and intuition.

I haven't included medium-ship because I do not work in that way. Even though I see and sense spirits, I do not pass messages on from the dearly departed. However, if you are seeking help in that area please visit my website for a list of contacts.

I hope you have enjoyed reading this book as much as I have enjoyed writing it. Enjoy your role as a light-worker in whatever capacity and please stay in touch.

Love Barbara x

Thanks to

Bruna Zanelli www.brunazanelli.com
Andrea Wren www.andreawren.co.uk
Deborah Wells www.deborahwells.co.uk
Michael Eardley www.noot54.co.uk
Ewa Griffiths www.seasidesoap.net/
Jacqui Metcalf www.inspiredpr.co.uk
Charlotte Robins www.purealternativetherapy.com
Angela Goodwin

BOOKS

6th Books investigates the paranormal, supernatural,
explainable or unexplainable. Titles cover everything included
within parapsychology: how to, lifestyles, beliefs, myths,
theories and memoir.